COMPASSIONATE SELF-CARE FOR NEW MOMS

MANAGE POSTPARTUM HEALTH, BOND WITH YOUR NEWBORN, NURTURE INNER CALM AND CHERISH THIS PRECIOUS TIME

SHARLENE HOSEK

TABLE OF CONTENTS

"Some Days I Am Goddess,
Some Days I Am Wild Child,
and
Some Days I Am a Fragile Mess.
Most Days I am a Bit of All Three.
But Every Day,
I Am Here,
Trying."

—S.C. Lourie

INTRODUCTION

Did you ever think that something as sublime as motherhood could make you question whether you could survive on coffee fumes and baby smiles? Welcome to the grand adventure of being a new mom, where the only constant is change, and your heart exists outside your body, probably wearing a diaper. You're not alone if you've found yourself whispering, "This is harder than I thought," amid those 3 a.m. feedings. But here's the sweet secret—nestled within this whirlwind of love and sleepless nights is the art of self-care, ready to be your new best friend.

This book, my dear reader, is my heart's work dedicated to you. It's not just any guide; it's a supportive hug, a knowing nod, and that reassuring voice saying, "You got this, mama." It's here to walk you through the transformative journey of new motherhood, empowering you to embrace your new identity with both arms and maybe a little bit of that baby drool. Because, let's face it, becoming a mom is nothing short of a superhero's origin story.

Now, let's get one myth out of the way: Self-care is not selfish. It's about ensuring that you are running on something other than empty. It's the oxygen mask principle—you must be breathing easy to keep things smooth sailing for your little one. This book is your guide to making self-care a non-negotiable part of your new life. This book is unique because it understands that not all self-care looks the same. Whether you recharge better alone or with others, there's a little toolbox of tips and tricks for every style.

From building emotional resilience to finding joy in the small moments, we'll explore a spectrum of strategies to prevent burnout and foster a deep, loving connection with yourself and your little one. And because I know your brain may be slightly mushier these days (hello, mommy brain), I've peppered this book with interactive elements like journal prompts, reflection exercises, and affirmations designed to bring more focus into your days and serenity into your nights.

Engage with this book actively. Scribble in the margins, answer the journal prompts honestly (grab a notebook if you want to keep all your answers in the same place), and let the affirmations remind you of your strength and worth. These interactive elements are your tools for carving out moments of peace and clarity throughout your day.

I invite you to dive into these pages with an open heart. Let this book be your daily companion, a source of comfort and inspiration as you navigate the adventure of new motherhood. My deepest wish is for you—through self-discovery and renewal—to finish this book feeling empowered, connected, and ready to face each day with renewed purpose and joy. Consider this book your cocoon, a safe space to grow, learn, and emerge prepared to soar. Motherhood may have turned your world upside down, but remember, butterflies only take flight after a period of transformation.

So, open your heart and mind, grab a cup of something nourishing or refreshing, and let's dive into this metamorphosis together. May this book be the supportive companion you need, offering comfort, laughter, and a gentle nudge toward embracing the beautiful, messy, extraordinary journey of motherhood.

With all my warmth and belief in your incredible strength,

Sharlene

CHAPTER ONE

ACKNOWLEDGING TRANSITION

I n motherhood, every day is a surprise party—you never quite know what will happen next. It's like building your adventure playground, where every piece is crafted from lessons learned and moments to treasure. Through this journey, transforming from woman to mother isn't just a phase; it's a deep dive into who you are, reshaping your essence and existence. This chapter explores the intricacy of adapting to motherhood, not by giving up the person you were but by weaving this monumental role into yet another layer of your identity.

The transition into motherhood is like the changing seasons, a natural and inevitable force, yet each phase brings unique experiences marked by distinct rhythms and intensities. Recognizing this transformation involves acknowledging the profound shifts happening both internally and externally. It's a transformation that touches every aspect of human emotion and physicality, reshaping the body and soul. By recognizing this, we permit ourselves to accept, without judgment, how our lives are adjusting to embrace our new roles. This acceptance is a crucial first step in understanding that the essence of self-care isn't found in resisting these changes but in adapting to them with flexibility and resilience.

The evolution of identity in new motherhood isn't about losing parts of your former self to make room for the mother within. It's more about growth, expanding your sense of self to include motherhood as a new facet of your identity. This concept is essential for personal growth and self-acceptance. It's about recognizing that the person who loved late-night movies, spontaneous trips, or long, uninterrupted reading sessions is still there, just in a new setting. This expanded identity welcomes the complexities and contradictions of motherhood, acknowledging that it's possible to feel both boundlessly joyful and profoundly exhausted, often at the same moment. In this acknowledgment, new moms can find peace with their evolving selves, realizing that growth often involves making room for this complexity.

Getting the hang of motherhood's twists and turns means packing a toolbox with self-compassion right at the center. It starts with realizing that adapting to motherhood isn't a straight line—it's more like a dance, with highs and lows, wins and challenges. Mindfulness is one handy tool that helps you embrace each moment without judgment. Then there's gratitude, which nudges your focus away from what's changed or missing to the richness that motherhood adds. Plus, keeping your expectations in check and understanding that productivity looks different now is key. These strategies, all steeped in self-compassion, smooth the path to embracing your new roles and responsibilities with more grace and much less pressure.

Being a new mom can be a constant frenzy of motion and emotion. It's easy for significant milestones to blend into the daily hustle of care and responsibilities. Yet, celebrating these milestones, whether giant leaps or small victories, is crucial for recognizing your progress and boosting your sense of achievement. Each milestone marks your resilience and ability to adapt, from nailing that first breastfeeding session to the joy of clocking a whole night's sleep. Celebrating can be as simple as pausing to soak in happiness or as festive as throwing a little family party. No matter how you celebrate, it's a powerful reminder of the value of your journey and the strength you've built along the way.

BRAIN DUMP

This book contains real-time questions that you can answer quickly within a few minutes. You can complete all the exercises as you progress through this book. But for now, learn the steps and take your time. Grab your notebook and let your brain clear.

Let's start with a practical step—diving into a Brain Dump, an exercise designed to empower you in navigating the myriad of thoughts, feelings, and priorities that accompany new motherhood. In this exercise, jot down every idea that arises, whether significant or trivial, a single word, a sentence, or a paragraph. Use the prompts to stimulate your thoughts and emotions, and as they emerge, record them without judgment or editing. The goal here isn't to categorize or structure these thoughts but to recognize their existence, offering a comprehensive overview of your present mental state. This book is your space for self-reflection and understanding.

Let's begin by answering, honestly and without editing, these following questions:

- Who loves me?
- Who do I love?
- Today, I feel …

- Today, I am grateful for …
- Today, my body feels… Today, my body needs…
- My top priority for this day is:
- What's on my mind (anything and everything):
- To boost my emotional health, today I am going to (perform the following actions):
- To improve my physical and mental well-being, today I am going to (perform the following actions):

THE ART OF LETTING GO

You are now a new mom. The once familiar paths of independence and spontaneity now feel like distant memories from another life. Many of us are not prepared for the unexpected sense of loss that this significant change brings. The sudden realization that a routine governed by naps and feedings has replaced the freedom to head out or enjoy an uninterrupted chat can weigh heavily on us. Recognizing this loss isn't a sign of ungratefulness but is instead a crucial part of adjusting to this new phase. It's about permitting ourselves to grieve the parts of our pre-motherhood lives that have been affected and, possibly, changed forever. These emotions are valid and understandable.

While adapting, your patience becomes a steadfast companion. This journey of reshaping your life around your new role comes with its fair share of challenges that test your stamina and grit. Here, patience is more than just riding out the storm; it's about actively participating in your transformation and recognizing that the evolution of your new identity isn't a sprint. It unfolds at its own pace, often surprising you when you least expect it. Patience gently reminds you that it's perfectly okay not to have all the answers right now, to feel swamped by the vastness of your new duties, or to miss pieces of your old life. It's about allowing yourself the room to trip up, pick up new lessons, and expand at your natural rhythm, free from the hurry-up pressure you often place on yourself. Remember, you are strong and capable; this experience is a testament to your resilience.

Alongside patience, self-compassion is a warm hug for your soul during those challenging moments of doubt and struggle. Just as you naturally offer understanding and kindness to a close friend braving the wild ride of new parenthood, you must extend that same gentleness to yourself. Self-compassion encourages you to swap self-criticism for empathy, to quiet the inner critic that doubts your abilities, and to celebrate your efforts with pride, no matter the results. It's about acknowledging that showing up daily for your child, yourself, and your family is a powerful display of your strength and love. Embracing self-compassion lays a strong foundation of confidence and acceptance in your evolving role as a parent. Remember, you are not alone in this journey; your feelings are valid and understood.

Our core values are the anchors that keep us steady as we navigate the twists and turns of change. Whether it's kindness, integrity, perseverance, or love, these values hold firm, shining even brighter as we step into motherhood. They help steer our choices and actions, reminding us of who we are at heart, beyond just being moms. These values shape how we view and react to our experiences, adding purpose and meaning to our journey and making each day more memorable.

Motherhood is transformative, shaping us into more complex and resourceful women. Affirmations are powerful declarations of our worth, capacity for love, and resilience. They are the gentle nudges we need on days when doubt clouds our vision, and they triumphantly cheer us on for the times we overcome fears. Each affirmation is a seed of positivity and strength planted in the nurturing soil of our hearts, where they take root and flourish. They might softly say, "I am enough," reinforcing our value amid chaos. Or they could boldly declare, "I embrace the fluidity of my emotions," recognizing the wide range of feelings that come with motherhood. They may also affirm, "My love is my strength," highlighting the deep connection that drives us forward. Each affirmation, though unique in its message, aims to bolster our self-belief, ignite self-acceptance, and light up our path with the glow of our inherent worth.

As you master the balance between letting go and holding on, you learn the true fluidity of motherhood isn't about achieving perfect balance but about the beauty of your earnest efforts. In the quiet moments of self-reflection, you whisper gentle words of encouragement to yourself, reaffirming your unwavering dedication to the core values that guide you. Within the haze of sleepless nights and seemingly endless days, you begin to see the silhouette of the woman you are becoming—not diminished by motherhood, but expanded, enriched, and enlivened by it. Remember, each step you take on this journey is a testament to your strength and the beauty that motherhood brings.

CELEBRATING YOUR BODY'S JOURNEY

The body is amazing. Think about it. Your body just grew a baby. It's wild. In postpartum recovery, where the body shows both the marks of challenge and triumph, the standard North American narrative often pushes for a rapid return to a pre-pregnancy physique as if erasing any sign of childbirth is the ultimate goal. This widespread perspective overlooks the incredible strength and endurance it takes to bring a new life into the world. Here lies a chance to change the conversation about postpartum bodies, moving away from rigid beauty standards to celebrate the body's remarkable ability to create and transform.

Body positivity invites us to see the physical changes brought by pregnancy and childbirth not as flaws to be corrected but as signs of a significant life event. It recognizes the body's adaptability and strength—traits that deserve more admiration than the pursuit of fitting arbitrary beauty standards. This view encourages new mothers to appreciate, not critique, what their bodies have achieved, affirming that the softness, the stretch marks, and the new shapes are not setbacks but badges of honor—visible tributes to the incredible feat they have accomplished. Your body, new mothers, is a testament to your experience, and it's time to celebrate it. Let's inspire each other to embrace our postpartum bodies and the power they represent.

The cultural obsession with getting back to a "pre-baby body" sets unrealistic expectations, imposing a one-size-fits-all recovery timeline that overlooks the unique journey of each woman. This pressure downplays the incredible work the body has done and shifts focus from what matters—health. It's time to steer the conversation from esthetics to well-being, recognizing that the postpartum period should be about healing and adjusting. True success during this time shouldn't be measured by how quickly someone fits back into their pre-pregnancy jeans but by how well they are healing overall—embracing practices that nourish the body, replenish energy, and support emotional health.

This shift in perspective sets the stage for developing self-care routines that celebrate rather than criticize the postpartum body. In this context, self-care goes beyond simple indulgence—it becomes a collection of deliberate actions that aid physical recovery and show appreciation for the body's resilience and strength. This could look like gentle exercises that help reconnect with one's physical self without the pressure of intense workouts or nutrition plans. It may also mean prioritizing rest and understanding that the body repairs itself during sleep. Each act of self-care, no matter how modest, is a tribute to the body's recovery process and a celebration of its enduring strength. By prioritizing self-care, you are taking control of your health and showing appreciation for your body's efficiency. You have the power to nurture your body and celebrate the incredible work it does every day.

HEART-TO-HEART

This next exercise is designed for deep introspection, empowering you to foster body positivity and support a health-focused recovery. It includes five reflective questions that examine your relationship with your postpartum body, encouraging you to honestly evaluate societal pressures to return to a "pre-baby body" and how these may have influenced your self-perception. When redefining body positivity for yourself, consider ways to support your body with kindness during recovery and reflect on unrealistic expectations you may currently face. By encouraging internal and external dialogue, this tool guides you toward a more nurturing relationship with your body, shifting your perspective to honor your body as deserving of care and respect, transcending societal standards.

Grab your notebook and, ideally, some extra time, and make some space for you. Perhaps, after you put your baby to sleep, find a quiet corner in your home where you can reflect without distractions and answer these questions:

1. How do you feel about your body since giving birth, considering all the changes it's gone through?

2. Can you recall any moment you felt proud or amazed by what your body has accomplished?

3. What does love and accepting your body mean to you now as a new mom?

4. What are some gentle ways to show kindness to your body as it heals and adjusts to motherhood?

5. What self-care practices bring you comfort and joy? How can you prioritize and make time for these practices amid the busyness of new motherhood?

BALANCING MOTHERHOOD AND PERSONAL GROWTH

Motherhood is like a caterpillar's transformation into a butterfly—complex and full of personal growth intertwined with nurturing a new life. There's this common myth about being the perfect mom who seems to handle everything flawlessly, keeping her kids and home spotless. Really? Let's be honest. The real scene is beautifully imperfect—filled with chaos, doubt, some tiredness, forgetfulness, and, let's face it, a touch of despair. Balancing personal growth and motherhood can be challenging, especially when juggling multiple responsibilities and meeting everyone's needs. Embracing these imperfections is the first step toward finding your balance. It takes time to mesh the new you with the old you into the role of mom.

Developing a positive mindset is crucial, helping you stay grounded in the present, where you can savor the small joys. Using mindfulness techniques allows you to tune in to the laughter, the tears, and those quiet moments with a sense of real presence that makes the daily chaos fade into the background. This mindset encourages you to treasure the present moments—like feeling the weight of your sleeping child against your chest or the warmth of their tiny hand in yours. It allows you to fully engage in the experiences of motherhood without becoming preoccupied with future worries or past regrets.

Setting realistic expectations is like venturing into new territory, knowing that things might change as you go. It means understanding that success in motherhood isn't always about ticking everything off your list or having a spotless house but rather about those special moments when you genuinely bond with your child, listening and responding with love even when you're busy. This approach reduces the pressure to meet impossible standards, making motherhood and personal growth more relaxed and forgiving. It acknowledges that progress isn't always linear, setbacks are part of the learning process, and every small effort helps deepen your understanding of yourself and your child.

Celebrating personal growth is about recognizing your journey through motherhood—the hurdles you've cleared and the resilience you've built along the way. It's about appreciating the strength in vulnerable moments, the lessons learned from mistakes, and the love that underpins even the most minor actions. This kind of celebration isn't about big gestures; it's deeply personal, a quiet nod to how you've grown as a person and a parent. In these moments of reflection, you truly see how much you've changed. It's not just about the significant milestones but also the subtle shifts in how you see things, your newfound patience, and the endless capacity for love that define what being a mom is all about. Celebrating personal growth can boost your self-esteem, increase your confidence, and help you feel more trusting in your parenting abilities.

Self-care routines are the backbone that keeps everything balanced, simple practices that nourish your body and soul. They don't need to be big or complicated—they fit right into your daily life, making them easy to keep up. Imagine doing a gentle stretch as dawn breaks, enjoying a hearty meal filled with laughs (and maybe a few spills), or taking a quiet moment to yourself under the stars. Each self-care act is a reminder that you're important and that taking care of yourself is as crucial as taking care of others. These routines improve your physical health and foster self-love, building a solid foundation supporting all facets of motherhood. Remember, self-care is not selfish; it's necessary for your overall health and scaffolds your ability to be the best mom you can be.

TRAIN YOUR ATTENTION

Here is a transformative mental exercise designed to enhance your ability to focus on one thing at a time. Practicing it can help shift your perspective toward what truly deserves your energy. By engaging in this exercise regularly, you can significantly reduce distractions and effectively direct your energy toward what's most important at any given moment. Regular practice also helps maintain lower stress levels and keeps you firmly grounded in the present. The power of focus allows us to resist the distractions that clutter our thoughts and dilute our daily experiences. Let's explore how this exercise can transform your focus and reduce stress.

1. **Choose Focus**: Select an object or sound to concentrate on. It could be the ticking of a clock, the sound of rain, the texture of a pen in your hand, or the shape of a book. Devote your complete attention to it. Notice its edges and color, see how much space it occupies, and feel its weight.
2. **Maintain Focus**: Keep your mind fixed on this focal point. If your thoughts wander—as they often will do—

gently guide them back without frustration or judgment.

3. **Self-Focus**: Once you feel your attention is fully immersed at 100 percent, intentionally shift your attention to yourself. Focus on your heart chakra (the energy center in your heart) and take one deep breath in and out. Feel yourself become grounded.

4. **Shift Focus**: Now, focus on another object or sound and concentrate on it. Devote your complete attention to it. Notice its edges, see how much space it occupies, feel its weight, and notice its color.

5. **Self-Focus**: Once you feel your attention is fully immersed at 100 percent, intentionally shift your attention to yourself. Focus on your heart chakra and take one deep breath in and out. Feel yourself become grounded.

6. **Repeat**: Continue this cycle of focusing and shifting your attention. This exercise will strengthen your mental "focus muscles," reducing distractions and amplifying your ability to remain entirely present. If you find yourself distracted, take a deep breath and refocus on your chosen object or sound. This practice is a powerful tool in training your mind to regulate where it directs its energy, giving you the power to control your thoughts and attention. Adequate time and practice help you regulate how much energy you give to something and how much energy you decide to hold back, empowering you to navigate your mental landscape with confidence.

7. **Keep Repeating**: Continue this process until you notice a significant improvement in your ability to direct your attention. Practice as frequently as desired, adapting it to suit your surroundings. You can use this exercise with individual senses such as listening, seeing,

feeling, tasting, and smelling. With enhanced proficiency, your ability to focus will become almost instantaneous. Once you hone in on something, channel your attention to that object (or situation) and allow everything else to fade into the background. Remember, with each repetition, you're strengthening your focus muscles and paving the way for deliberate experiences and a less stressful life.

Over time, this practice helps set priorities, establish boundaries, and conserve energy while deepening your connection with the present moment, your child, and yourself. As your attention sharpens and your mental resilience builds, you can use this technique to avoid unhelpful or negative thoughts, situations, and even people. You can choose experiences that promote self-love and make your day more joyful.

As we close this chapter on embracing the new facets of motherhood, it's essential to hold dear the art of letting go, the celebration of your body's remarkable journey, and the balancing act between personal growth and motherhood. Letting go teaches us to release our pre-motherhood expectations and embrace our new reality gracefully. Celebrating your body acknowledges the incredible process it has undergone, honoring its strength and resilience. Meanwhile, balancing motherhood with personal growth involves recognizing that this new role doesn't diminish who you are but enriches your identity profoundly. Each aspect— letting go, celebrating, and balancing—contributes to a more harmonious experience of motherhood, where self-compassion and personal evolution go hand in hand. As you continue this journey, remember that each step, no matter how small, is a part of your growth into a wise, loving, and resilient mother.

CHAPTER TWO

THE HEARTBEAT OF SELF-CARE

The morning sun pours through the window, filling the room with a warm glow. It's a new day, but that to-do list from yesterday has yet to get any shorter, and it seems to grow daily. Between the non-stop feedings, diaper changes, and snatch-and-grab naps, finding time for self-care can seem elusive. Yet, it's precisely during moments of overwhelm that self-care becomes vitally important. Taking time for self-care provides a mother with more energy and empowers her to care for her child and her own spirit with more patience and much more grace. It's a small investment that yields significant returns.

Self-care shifts from a luxury to a necessity once you recognize that taking care of yourself is just as important as taking care of your family. It's that deep breath before you plunge back into parenting, the quiet moment of reflection that lets patience and kindness triumph over frustration and exhaustion. This change in perspective is like realizing that watering the roots benefits the whole tree, ensuring it remains strong and vibrant to provide shade and fruit. As such, within this space lies the possibility of choice. It's easy to react when we find ourselves in the thick of things. Being caught up, we move automatically, getting things done. How much do we do? Why, all of it, of course. Or as much as our overloaded selves can handle, and then some.

If you ever feel overwhelmed, it's okay to pause for a moment. Seriously, stop everything. Stand still, close your eyes, and take a slow, deep breath. A one-second breath to pause. Breathe in deeply again, slowly letting it out. This little break is your space to think before you act. Now, gently think about what single task you must focus on. Great. Next, think about the first step you must take to start or complete this task. Ready? Go ahead and take that step. Once done, calmly decide what comes next and repeat the process for the next task. Remember, learning to manage your mental space and focusing on one thing at a time isn't just productive—it's a form of caring for yourself. Take it one step at a time.

Prioritizing your needs isn't selfish; it's a profoundly responsible act. It means acknowledging when your energy is running low or your mind is frazzled and taking the time to ground yourself. Give yourself a moment of your precious time to ensure you remain physically and emotionally present. You can instantly recharge with a deep breath in and out—a one-second pause to reset. In this space, define your next move. Respond, don't react. Ask yourself, "What is the most important thing right now?" Acknowledge the answer and let everything else fade from your mental awareness. Deliberately decide your next step. It's important to manage your energy output and conserve your reserves until you can replenish them, especially as you navigate the complex emotions that often accompany self-care.

Guilt can overshadow the pursuit of self-care, casting doubts and magnifying fears. It's a common misconception that self-care takes away from family time, branding it as a selfish indulgence. Now is the time to rewrite this narrative. Self-care isn't about subtracting from family care; self-care enhances it. It's essential to establish clear boundaries and empower yourself with open conversations with your family about why these self-care practices are not only beneficial but necessary. Integrating self-care into your family's daily routine transforms it from a solitary act into a shared value, enriching the collective well-being. When you prioritize your well-being, you model healthy habits and resilience for your family, fostering an environment where everyone's needs are respected and nurtured. Remember, self-care isn't selfish; it's a vital component to maintaining balance, strength, and harmony within yourself and your family unit.

Regular self-care brings a treasure trove of long-term benefits beyond the here and now. For new moms, dedicating time to self-care is a game changer—it helps keep mental health in check, warding off postpartum depression and easing anxiety by offering well-deserved breaks and a chance to recharge emotionally. Physically, it's just as mighty, helping to improve sleep quality, reduce inflammation, and boost immune function, all essential as your body heals after childbirth. But the perks don't stop there—self-care helps you hold on to your sense of self and boosts personal fulfillment. These practices build resilience, allowing you to handle life's ups and downs gracefully. By putting your well-being on the priority list, you're setting yourself up for continued energy and a more optimistic life perspective, enriching your overall life experience in vibrant ways.

DEFINE YOUR PRIORITIES

Picture a typical Wednesday. You've just put the baby down for a nap, giving you a precious thirty-minute break before things pick up again. Now, you're at a crossroads—you could dive into that ever-growing laundry pile, scroll through social media, or pick a self-care activity to boost your energy. This ordinary moment is an excellent opportunity to bring the ideas from this chapter into action. It's a chance to put your well-being first, realizing that a quick walk (around the house counts) or a few minutes of meditation (sitting with a cup of tea and staring at the wall counts) can change the tone of your entire day and improve how you respond to your family's needs, giving you more patience. Remarkably, when you choose yourself first, you simultaneously prioritize others. When you create space for you, you also create space for them. Making this choice consistently over time becomes a strong affirmation of self-care's importance, helping you break free from guilt and redefine what it means to be a caring, present parent and spouse.

By embracing self-care, we rewrite the narrative of motherhood from one defined by sacrifice and exhaustion to one brimming with balance, health, and joy. This transformation begins with each individual but carries the power to reshape families, communities, and even future generations. It plants the seeds for a future where caring for oneself is understood as the essential basis for caring for others.

At the heart of self-care is self-awareness. It's about asking yourself, "How can I show kindness to myself in this moment?" Maybe instead of carrying five bags of groceries all at once, it's taking two bags and returning for the rest. Maybe it's not answering the phone right away because you're feeling stressed, and the best thing you can do for your anxiety level is to let that person go and call them when you've settled down. It could be dropping the world and spending bonding time with your little one all day and not feeling the least bit guilty about it at all. It could be making dinner in the morning, so you have all afternoon free. It could be that you spontaneously need a change of scenery and go for a half-hour random drive during your baby's naptime, like today.

Whenever you are feeling overwhelmed, confused, or simply exhausted, return to this fundamental question. Recognize that within you lies the wisdom to answer this question, providing insight into the self-care your body craves in the present moment. Listen to this answer, modifying it if necessary or postponing it for later. But most importantly, acknowledge that this answer exists. This self-awareness, this understanding of your needs, will serve as your compass, guiding you toward greater well-being.

Repeat your new mantra. "How can I be kind to myself right now?"

UNDERSTANDING PERSONALITY TYPES

Everyone's motherhood journey is unique in that each mom's traits shape her experience. Understanding different personality types—introverts, extroverts, and refined ambiverts—can revolutionize self-care strategies. Each personality type has strengths and challenges that influence how moms approach motherhood and self-care, tailoring their routines to meet their needs. Recognizing these differences is key. Whether you recharge in quiet solitude or draw energy from being around others, getting to know your personality type can help you craft a self-care routine that fits just right. This personalized approach allows every mom to support her journey effectively, blending the right mix of energy and tranquility to enhance well-being in natural and fulfilling ways.

Those cherished moments of quiet contemplation might feel rare for the introverted mama. Introverts thrive on moments of deep reflection, where the world slows down just enough to hear their thoughts above the baby babble. Introverted people tend to be reflective, reserved, independent, thoughtful, and observant. The real challenge for introverted moms is finding those little pockets of peace in the whirlwind of a baby. Do your best to create a tiny oasis of tranquility in your day where you can sneak away for a breath (or gulp) of fresh air and a moment to reconnect with your inner calm. Trust me, even just a few stolen seconds can work wonders for an introvert's energy and patience levels.

Conversely, extroverts are like energy magnets, drawing their vitality from the bustling world around them. They thrive on lively interactions and the vibrant exchange of energy with others. Extroverts tend to be sociable, outgoing, collaborative, action-oriented, and expressive. The challenge is that early motherhood can sometimes feel like being stranded on a deserted island. As the social circle shrinks, you must get creative with your connections. Redefine what hanging out means and identify early on the people whom you can turn to, even if it's just for a brief chat. Remember, even those quick connections can be a lifeline during this transformative time.

TAILORED SELF-CARE STRATEGIES

Introverted self-care ideas:

1. Carve out quiet time to read a book or sip a warm drink.
2. Write in a journal to process thoughts and feelings.
3. Take a peaceful solo stroll around the neighborhood while the baby sleeps in the stroller.
4. DIY project during those rare moments of downtime.
5. Indulge in a bath (a short one counts) with soothing music or a calming podcast playing in the background.

6. Sneak in a short meditation or stretch session.
7. Cook a favorite meal to treat yourself.
8. Create a cozy nook at home with soft blankets and dim lighting.
9. Watch a movie or catch up on a TV show.
10. Set aside some time to unplug from screens and unwind.

Extroverted self-care ideas:

1. Host a virtual coffee date with other new mom friends to chat and catch up.
2. Join online parenting groups or forums to connect with other moms sharing similar experiences.
3. Participate in virtual classes or challenges with a supportive community.
4. Organize a fun-themed virtual game night with friends for laughs and camaraderie.
5. Attend live-streamed concerts or performances from the comfort of your home.
6. Plan a future outing or day trip with other moms and their little ones.
7. Volunteer for a cause or organization that resonates with your values.
8. Organize an outdoor picnic or park hangout with other family members.
9. Attend parenting workshops for social interaction and learning. Some places have baby care (within your view) while you attend the meeting.
10. Schedule regular phone or video calls with friends and family members for connection and support.

Between introverts and extroverts, we find the ambivert, dancing between the two worlds with effortless grace. Like a social chameleon, they draw energy from solitude and lively gatherings, adjusting quickly to whatever situation they find themselves in. Ambiverts tend to be flexible, balanced, empathetic, versatile, and adaptable. The challenge for them lies in finding that perfect harmony of quiet moments and social adventures so that both their introverted and extroverted sides feel nourished and fulfilled. One challenge ambiverts may encounter is difficulty prioritizing their needs, leading them to overextend themselves. It's essential to identify your priorities and set boundaries to prevent your energy levels from flatlining, leaving you feeling depleted. Embracing this balance ensures that ambiverts can navigate life with authenticity, resilience, and contentment.

Amid the diaper changes and sleepless nights, prioritizing self-care becomes essential. Regardless of your unique journey, there are fundamental aspects of self-care that all new mothers can benefit from. First and foremost is taking care of your physical well-being. Adding exercise and healthy eating to your routine can boost your energy levels, helping you manage the demands of motherhood. Equally important is nurturing your emotional health. Finding ways to cultivate stability and foster joy can make a world of difference in navigating the ups and downs of parenting. And let's not overlook the importance of practical self-care. By organizing your environment and managing your time effectively, you can reduce stress and boost efficiency, helping you better handle the demands of your new role. Remember, self-care isn't selfish—it's a necessary part of being the best mom you can be. So, be kind to yourself and prioritize your well-being as you spread your wings and gracefully navigate this beautiful journey of motherhood.

As your little one grows, the self-care scene undergoes a transformation, demanding flexibility and creativity. The routines that kept you sane during those sleep-deprived newborn days will need a makeover to adapt to your child's changing needs. Think of it as a dance, a fun, sometimes clumsy, but constantly evolving rhythm of figuring things out as you go. One thing remains constant through all the adjustments and surprises—self-care is your trusty sidekick. Remember to be flexible yet remain steady in carving out a few minutes (or more) each day to focus on watering the tree. Your self-care is not just a luxury; it's a necessity. It's a way of showing yourself that you are valued and understood.

THE MYTH OF DOING IT ALL: SETTING REALISTIC EXPECTATIONS

Each day begins with joyful surprises, creating a scene that is far more vibrant and animated than the stereotypical "perfect mom." This illusion, stitched together from societal pressures, glossy magazines, and perfectly posed social media snapshots, paints an image of motherhood that's as dazzling as it is unreachable. It whispers tales of pristine homes, gourmet meals, and tranquil babies, all handled with the grace of a ballerina by a mother who never skips a beat. Yet, beneath this glossy exterior lies the raw, beautiful truth of motherhood—it's a wonderfully messy, utterly exhausting adventure that refuses to stick to a script.

The first step in shattering the myth of "doing it all" is to tackle the notion of perfection directly, questioning its actual worth and attainability. Perfection is, by nature, a constantly moving target, shifting with every new fad, opinion, or milestone. Trying to achieve this ideal is like tackling an endless task—it takes away the joy and spontaneity that make motherhood so special. Instead, we must focus on setting realistic goals that recognize the complexities of life with a new baby and the limited nature of time and energy. Dismissing the ideal does not concede defeat; it's a celebration of authenticity, acknowledging that giving your best effort is enough.

The true charm of motherhood isn't captured in picture-perfect Instagram snapshots but in everyday life's beautifully flawed, unscripted moments. It's in the laughter that escapes during a milk spill, the comfort of a baby blanket, and the soothing warmth of a cuddle that melts away the weariness of a sleepless night. To embrace these imperfections is to stage a rebellion against the myth of the perfect mom, proclaiming that the chaos of motherhood is not just okay—it's utterly beautiful. In these messy, real moments, you weave memories, strengthen bonds, and let the genuine spirit of family life glow the brightest.

While setting realistic expectations, mastering the art of goal-setting is key. Achievable goals include understanding the unpre-dictable rhythm of life with a newborn and recognizing that some days, success might simply mean feeding the baby, catching a quick shower, or snatching a few precious hours of sleep. On other days, it could be enjoying a cup of tea while it's still warm, taking a short walk to refresh your mind, or successfully soothing your baby with a new lullaby. These aren't signs of settling; they're thoughtful decisions to prioritize well-being over a never-ending to-do list. These small victories are significant milestones in the daily life of a mother. These goals offer flexibility and adaptability, and most importantly, they provide the chance to celebrate each small victory, adding up to a fulfilling day. By embracing achievable goals, mothers can move through their days feeling accomplished and not constantly behind.

THE POWER OF SAYING NO

In a world where being continuously busy is often mistaken for being worthy, saying no becomes a powerful tool for setting realistic expectations. No is a word that sets boundaries, safeguarding your time, energy, and emotional health. Embracing the power to decline is not about being uncooperative; it's about recognizing that not every invitation, request, or expectation is practical or desirable, particularly during the demanding initial months of motherhood. It's a declaration that the well-being of both mom and baby is more important than any external pressures, whether from family, friends, or societal norms. Saying no isn't selfish—it's an act of self-care, ensuring that your reserves are never depleted and that there's always plenty to offer to those who matter most. This is especially crucial in motherhood, where your overall health directly impacts your ability to care for your baby.

To empower yourself in setting and maintaining realistic expectations, consider creating your own "Yes/No!" worksheet. Start by jotting down everything currently on your plate—your to-do lists, social invitations, and various tasks. Then, evaluate each item for both desire and feasibility. Respond decisively with Yes or No. If you're unsure, label it as Maybe. This placeholder serves as a reminder that it's a potential commitment you can revisit when you have more time and energy. This process clarifies what truly needs your attention and strengthens your ability to set clear boundaries. By visualizing your commitments on paper, you can better identify what is consuming your energy and what genuinely deserves your focus.

For each question you answered Yes to, consider setting a target completion date. Remember, this date isn't set in stone; you can adjust it to suit your current circumstances. Allow yourself the flexibility to change your mind, postpone tasks, or accelerate your progress based on what's best for you, given the constraints of your current life. By creating this worksheet, you free up mental space and improve your ability to focus on your true priorities, ensuring that you invest your time and energy wisely.

With time and practice, you will be able to mentally assess which situations deserve your commitment and which are better to walk away from. By deliberately choosing your priorities, you respond rather than react to your external and internal environments. Knowing how much you are willing to give, which directly ties to how much energy you actually have, can be liberating. When you prioritize your choices, you naturally conserve energy, leaving more for yourself, your baby, and your spouse. And with more energy, guess what? You also gain more patience. It's a win-win situation all around.

As moms progress through the parenting journey, where the ideal often veers from reality, the tale of "doing it all" gently steps aside. In its place, a story woven with integrity, authenticity, and abundance emerges. This version cheers on the charm of imperfection, the smarts of manageable goals, and the power of knowing when to say no. Realistic expectations are at the heart of this approach. It's a gentle reminder that the only expectations that truly matter are the ones you set for yourself, and, in doing so, you shape your own fulfilling and personalized experiences.

SELF-CARE IN 15 MINUTES: QUICK WINS FOR BUSY MOMS

It's easy to trip over the myth that self-care demands hours of free time to truly refresh. But here's a cheerful truth: a splash of creativity and a dash of intention can transform even a quick five minutes into a peaceful retreat. The secret isn't finding more time —it's all about weaving self-care into the natural rhythm of your daily life, turning those moments into golden opportunities for rejuvenation. So, let's not wait for free hours that never come; let's sprinkle a little self-care magic throughout our day right where we are!

Here are twenty quick and easy self-care strategies for busy moms:

1. Strap on a baby carrier and take a brisk walk outside, enjoying the fresh air and a change of scenery.
2. While feeding or cuddling your baby, take deep, slow breaths to help calm your mind and body. Hum a tune or sing.
3. Put on some of your favorite music and have a mini dance party.
4. Listen to an audiobook or podcast while doing chores or relaxing with your baby.
5. Do light stretching or gentle exercises while keeping eye contact and engaging with your baby on their play mat.
6. Spend a few minutes acknowledging things that you are grateful for.
7. Prepare some healthy snacks for yourself to have quick and nutritious options.
8. Keep a water bottle with you and place several throughout the house to ensure you stay hydrated.
9. Send a quick text or make a short call to a friend for a brief catch-up.
10. Organize your baby photos, send some to print, and have them delivered to your home, all from the convenience of your phone.
11. Try a 5-minute guided meditation or deep breathing session for relaxation. Or stare out of the window (hopefully at some nature).

12. Spend a few minutes reading a magazine, comic book, or whatever material brings you joy.
13. Engage in a simple craft like knitting or crocheting, which you can easily pick up and put down.
14. Use a face mask or indulge in a quick pamper session while your baby is content or sleeping.
15. Soak up some sunshine to boost your mood and vitamin D levels.
16. Learn something new, like a crafting technique or a cooking skill, in small, manageable increments.
17. Give yourself a foot soak or a hand massage to relax and unwind.
18. Savor a cup of herbal tea or your favorite healthy snack as a quick treat.
19. Write down one thing you've accomplished today, no matter how small, to acknowledge your daily achievements.
20. Set a timer for 15 minutes and do something you enjoy guilt-free, whether reading, scrolling through social media, or sitting quietly.

These are some examples. Be sure to design your strategies to be easily incorporated into your busy day, giving you a quick pick-me-up whenever you need it most!

QUICK RELAXATION TECHNIQUES

Among the many self-care strategies, relaxation techniques are particularly convenient for their immediate impact on mental and emotional well-being. Take deep breathing exercises, for example. They provide a direct path to calm, grounding your mind and body with each deliberate inhale and exhale. This straightforward yet powerful practice can be done anywhere, whether it's the brief solitude of a locked bathroom or the quiet of a child's bedroom. Consider adding a quick gratitude practice to your daily routine. At the start or end of each day, pause to reflect on one thing you are grateful for. It could be simple joys like a warm hug from your child, a moment of laughter shared with a friend, or even a delicious meal enjoyed together as a family. Cultivating gratitude can shift your focus from stressors to blessings, fostering a positive mindset and enhancing overall well-being.

Similarly, guided visualizations, readily available through various apps, transport the mind to tranquil landscapes, providing an immediate respite from the day's stresses. These practices, both easy to perform and profoundly beneficial, are keys to unlocking moments of peace amid daily activities. Think of who loves you and who you love. Cultivating affection and caring into your thought pattern enhances your ability to cope with stress. It nurtures a sense of emotional well-being that radiates into your daily life.

Affirmations are powerful tools for boosting your mental and emotional well-being, reminding you of your strength, resilience, and worth, particularly when uncertain or stressed. These positive statements can be tailored to suit your specific needs or goals, acting like a bit of light in times of weariness or discouragement. Whether you whisper them to yourself in the morning, take a moment to reflect on them during a break in your day, or think about them before bed, each repetition helps reinforce their uplifting messages in your mind. Affirmations like "I am doing my best, and that is enough" or "At this moment, I choose calm" act as gentle nudges of self-compassion, aiding in maintaining a positive outlook and building lasting inner strength.

As we progress, remember that self-care is more than just a lofty goal—it's a practical, essential part of our daily routine. By seizing quick, meaningful victories and embracing moments of mindfulness, we affirm our worth, refresh our spirits, and enhance the lives of those around us. This strategy helps us develop a daily routine that is both nourishing and sustainable, improving our experience of motherhood and everything that accompanies it.

FINDING OPPORTUNITIES

Opportunities for self-care are hidden in the ordinary moments of daily life, waiting for those keen enough to spot them. They can be found in the quiet of the early morning before anyone else is awake, in the soothing swirls of steam rising from a hot cup of tea, and even in the rhythmic comfort of folding laundry. Recognizing these moments means shifting how we view our everyday routines—being open to finding mindfulness in the simplest tasks. It involves transforming bath time from a routine chore into a session of playful splashes and relaxation or turning a regular walk to the park into a chance for exercise and reconnection with nature. This flexibility is crucial when incorporating self-care into the busy life of a mom, as adhering too rigidly to plans can often add stress rather than alleviate it.

A flexible approach to self-care adapts to the unpredictable tides of parenting, accommodating the natural ups and downs of energy and time. This means having a toolbox of practical, quick self-care strategies ready, perfect for fitting into a brief five-minute break or expanding into more extended periods when the opportunity arises. This adaptability ensures that self-care is a constant, empowering you and remaining a tangible part of your life.

The true transformative power of self-care lies not in grand, sporadic gestures but in the cumulative effect of small, consistent acts of kindness toward oneself. Regularly incorporating these quick self-care rituals into your daily routine transforms them from luxuries to indispensable elements of everyday well-being. Consistency becomes a habit, and over time, these habits become second nature, seamlessly blending self-care into the fabric of daily life. This regular practice fortifies resilience, equipping mothers with the inner strength to meet parenting challenges with grace and vitality.

As we wrap up, view your journey into motherhood as an adventure where each day brings a new opportunity to learn, evolve, and love a little more. It's not about getting everything right but about cherishing the connections you forge, the small discoveries you make about yourself, and about nurturing your little one and yourself. Always remember that you're doing an incredible job, and this book is here as a supportive friend—ready to help and remind you that you're not alone in this. So, here's to embracing the beautiful chaos of motherhood, growing alongside your child, and savoring the wonderfully rich life you're building together. Cheers to you, Mom—step by confident step.

CHAPTER THREE

POSTPARTUM RECOVERY— WHAT TO EXPECT

Just as a garden in spring is a time of new beginnings and renewal, so too is becoming a new mom. Your postpartum health progresses through various stages of recovery, and your experience is unique, reflecting your individual physical and emotional needs. Recognizing and supporting these differences among mothers is essential to ensure you receive the best care for your situation. Initially, the body starts a healing journey from childbirth, which spans from the immediate hours after delivery to several weeks later. During this early stage, the focus is on the body's immediate response to childbirth, from the uterus contracting back to its pre-pregnancy size to healing any tears or incisions made during delivery. This period is a critical time of transition, signaling the start of recovery as the body adapts and begins to restore itself.

As the weeks turn into months, the recovery process shifts from primarily physical healing to encompass hormonal rebalancing and adapting to the physical demands of caring for a newborn. Hormonal fluctuations influence everything from mood swings to skin and hair texture. Additionally, the body's shape transforms, gradually shedding the physical signs of pregnancy and adapting to a new normal. For many women, this process is both bewildering and awe-inspiring, highlighting the body's remarkable capacity to adapt and change.

As the body navigates the dual challenges of recovery and motherhood, energy levels may fluctuate dramatically. While this phase may be less intense physically, it still requires a sustained commitment to nurturing one's health and well-being. This ongoing dedication helps ensure the postpartum recovery journey is as smooth and supported as possible.

Breast changes are particularly notable for those who opt to breastfeed. Challenges such as engorgement, sensitivity, and learning the proper breastfeeding techniques can present physical and emotional hurdles. Additionally, there is also postpartum bleeding and the gradual cessation of lochia—the discharge that occurs after childbirth. Open discussion of these topics helps demystify the natural processes the body undergoes during recovery, offering crucial knowledge and reassurance to new mothers as they navigate these changes.

Establishing a universal timeline for postpartum recovery is as unpredictable as forecasting the weather—while there are general patterns that can be anticipated, the specifics are deeply personal. Some may experience a swift recovery, quickly returning to a sense of "normalcy," while others may find it a slower process, gently rediscovering their body at its own pace. This timeline doesn't adhere to strict boundaries and is influenced by various factors, including the nature of the delivery, any pre-existing health conditions, and the level of support available. Each mother's experience is unique, reflecting the individual nature of both birth and recovery.

As you navigate postpartum recovery, guidance from healthcare professionals provides direction and reassurance. It's crucial to be vigilant for issues that may require medical attention, such as excessive bleeding, signs of infection, or significant mood changes that could indicate postpartum depression. This vigilance, far from causing alarm, is a wise component of informed care, ensuring that any issues are addressed promptly and effectively to support a healthy recovery.

VAGINAL DELIVERY

During a vaginal birth, a woman's body undergoes significant transformations. It faces numerous challenges, including the process of labor, the actual birth of the child, and the expulsion of the placenta. The initial phase involves contractions that progressively dilate the cervix, making it possible for the baby to descend into the birth canal, a process that can be quite painful and is usually the longest. The second phase sees the mother experiencing a strong urge to push with each contraction, aiding the baby's journey through the birth canal and into the world, often accompanied by a burning feeling as the baby stretches the vaginal tissues. The final phase entails the delivery of the placenta, during which it is critical to ensure that all remnants are removed to avert complications such as postpartum hemorrhage.

Complications during delivery can include excessive bleeding, tears in the vaginal area or the perineum, and prolonged labor, which may necessitate medical interventions. An episiotomy, for example, is a surgical cut made in the perineum—the tissue between the vaginal opening and the anus—to enlarge the vaginal opening and facilitate the delivery of the baby. This procedure is typically performed under local anesthesia and is intended to prevent more severe natural tears and control the direction and extent of the tearing.

Healthcare providers may use assistive devices to help deliver the baby when there are complications, such as fetal distress or stalled labor. In rare cases, assistive devices include forceps and vacuum extractors. Forceps are curved instruments that fit around the baby's head, allowing the healthcare provider to guide the baby out during a contraction. A vacuum extractor uses a soft cup attached to the baby's head, connected to a pump that creates suction, helping to guide the baby down the birth canal during contractions. These interventions are used to safely expedite delivery and minimize risk to both the mother and the baby, especially in urgent situations where the baby needs to be delivered quickly or the mother is unable to push effectively.

During childbirth, a woman's body undergoes a series of intense physical experiences. Sweating is expected as the body exerts itself during labor, similar to any strenuous physical activity. Fatigue sets in as the labor can last for many hours, requiring sustained physical effort and endurance. Women often experience significant pain from contractions and the process of the baby moving through the birth canal, which can lead to feelings of fear or anxiety about the process and its outcomes. Hormonal changes during labor also intensify emotions and physical sensations, contributing to an overwhelming experience that requires immense physical and emotional resilience.

As this intense phase concludes, the focus shifts to postpartum recovery, which involves a period of both physical and emotional healing. Physically, the body repairs tissues and organs displaced during pregnancy and delivery, with the uterus returning to its pre-pregnancy size within about six weeks and perineal tears healing over a similar period. Women often experience discomfort, swelling, and post-delivery bleeding for several weeks.

C-SECTIONS

When a new mom comes home after a cesarean section, commonly known as a C-section, she's beginning a recovery process that differs from a vaginal delivery. A C-section is a major surgery in which a baby is delivered through cuts made in the mother's abdomen and uterus. Postpartum recovery involves managing pain, understanding the surgery's impact, and knowing how to care for oneself while adjusting to life with a new baby.

In the first few weeks after a C-section, a mom can expect several types of discomfort. Pain at the incision site is common, and it may feel sharp or burn a bit, especially when moving. The abdomen may feel sore and tender as it heals, and some women experience cramping as the uterus shrinks back to its pre-pregnancy size. It's also expected to feel pain or discomfort from gas and bloating after surgery due to air introduced into the abdomen during the procedure.

The healing process for a C-section typically lasts about six weeks, but this can vary. During this time, it's important to watch for signs that might warrant a call to the doctor, such as increased redness, swelling, or leaking from the incision site, which could indicate infection. Fever, severe pain that doesn't improve with medication, and heavy bleeding are also reasons to seek medical advice.

New moms should focus on resting and bonding with their babies at home without overexerting themselves. It's important to avoid lifting anything heavier than the baby and to avoid strenuous activities that strain the incision area. Walking around the house is encouraged, as it promotes healing and helps prevent blood clots.

Moms can expect some bleeding from the vagina, known as lochia, even after a C-section. This is the body's way of getting rid of the extra blood and tissue that helps the baby grow. Bleeding should gradually decrease, but contacting a healthcare provider is necessary if it gets heavier or contains large clots.

Managing self-care involves being gentle with oneself. It's crucial to follow the doctor's instructions on how to care for the incision, keep it clean, and recognize signs of possible complications. It's important to manage discomfort during recovery, and taking prescribed pain medication can be helpful. If you're breastfeeding, always check with your healthcare provider before taking any medication.

During this time, moms should also ensure they have support at home. Helping with household chores and meals, as well as caring for the baby, can give the mom more time to rest and recover. Emotionally, it's a time of significant adjustment, so support from partners, family, or friends can also help new moms navigate this challenging yet joyful time.

Overall, a C-section is a significant surgical procedure, and giving the body time to heal while managing pain and watching for signs of complications is critical to a healthy recovery. Remember, every mom's recovery experience is unique, and consulting with healthcare providers about any concerns is essential.

THE RECOVERY PERIOD

Your emotions during the postpartum period can range from joy to anxiety, with many mothers experiencing frequent mood swings due to large hormonal fluctuations. If these symptoms worsen or persist beyond two weeks, it could indicate postpartum depression, necessitating professional help. New mothers should seek medical attention for severe pain, heavy bleeding, fever, or signs of infection, as these may point to more serious complications.

A follow-up appointment is typically scheduled six weeks after delivery, but complications or concerns may warrant earlier visits. The postpartum period is a crucial time for self-care, with mothers encouraged to rest, maintain a balanced diet, and seek support from their network or health professionals to ensure a smooth recovery.

The range of postpartum discomfort includes everything from the physical strains of labor to the subtler adjustments of a changing body. Breastfeeding, while fostering a deep bond between mother and child, can introduce challenges like mastitis or sore nipples, often catching new mothers off guard with their intensity. Recovery from surgical procedures such as episiotomies or cesarean sections adds another dimension of discomfort, necessitating careful attention and patience as incisions heal. Additionally, routine tasks like holding a newborn for extended periods or frequent bending during diaper changes can lead to back pain, subtly underscoring the physical demands of motherhood. Awareness and preparation for these various forms of postpartum discomfort can significantly aid in managing them effectively, allowing new mothers to focus more on healing and bonding with their little ones.

Natural Pain Management Techniques

As you manage your postpartum recovery, exploring natural pain relief methods can be incredibly beneficial. Warm compresses are great for easing sore spots by gently alleviating tenderness.

Sitz baths are particularly beneficial for reducing swelling and aiding healing in the perineal area, which often becomes sore and inflamed after childbirth. Additionally, warm showers can also relax tense muscles, offering a comforting and calming experience.

Staying hydrated is crucial for postpartum recovery. It helps maintain the balance of bodily fluids, aids in digestion, and supports overall health. Sipping herbal teas, such as ginger or chamomile, can naturally ease discomfort thanks to their soothing properties. If you're experiencing back pain, incorporating gentle postpartum stretching exercises into your routine can be beneficial. These exercises, designed specifically for new moms, aim to gently and effectively strengthen and stretch your body.

Heating pads can be incredibly beneficial for new moms, providing relief from various postpartum discomforts. Heat therapy increases blood flow to the area where the heat is applied. This enhanced circulation helps to relax and soothe muscles, reduce stiffness, and alleviate pain. Specifically, for new mothers, heating pads can be particularly effective in easing pain from childbirth-related muscle strains, cramping, and general soreness. They can also help with back pain, which is common during the postpartum period due to the strain of carrying and breastfeeding a newborn.

When using a heating pad, it's important to follow some basic safety guidelines to avoid skin burns or other injuries.

1. **Check the temperature.** Start with the lowest heat setting and gradually increase it to find a comfortable level. The heat should feel warm but not uncomfortably hot.

2. **Use a barrier.** Place a cloth or towel between the heating pad and the skin to prevent direct contact and reduce the risk of burns.

3. **Limit time.** Avoid using the heating pad on any area for more than 20 minutes at a time. Extended heat application can cause burns or even increase inflammation.

4. **Stay alert.** Do not use the heating pad while sleeping. It's essential to be fully aware in case the heat becomes too intense.

5. **Avoid damaged skin.** Do not apply heat to areas where the skin is broken, bruised, or swollen, as this could exacerbate the condition.

For new moms, heating pads can be used on the lower back, abdomen, or other areas that may be sore from labor and delivery or from holding and nursing a newborn. When choosing a heating pad, selecting one with a timed automatic shut-off feature and controlled temperature settings is a safety measure that enhances your peace of mind. This design ensures the pad turns off automatically after a set period, preventing overheating and reducing the risk of burns if you accidentally fall asleep or forget to turn it off. Adjustable temperature controls allow you to set the heat to a comfortable level, making it easier to use the pad safely without constantly monitoring it. These features provide reassurance and make the heating pad more user-friendly, especially for new moms who may be dealing with frequent distractions or exhaustion. Always ensure the heating pad is in good working condition and follow the manufacturer's instructions for use.

Using ice in postpartum care, particularly after an episiotomy or a perineal tear, helps manage pain and reduce swelling by constricting blood vessels and decreasing inflammation. It can also numb the area, providing immediate relief. It's important to wrap ice packs in a cloth or use commercial cold packs designed for body use to prevent frostbite and skin damage. Typically, ice should be applied in short intervals, no more than twenty minutes at a time, with breaks in between to prevent skin damage and discomfort. This careful application ensures that the benefits of cold therapy are maximized without any adverse effects, providing targeted relief as part of a comprehensive postpartum recovery plan.

Massage therapy can be highly effective in promoting relaxation and improving circulation, which aids in the healing process. It can help reduce muscle tension, improve lymphatic drainage, and increase the production of endorphins, which are natural painkillers. Exploring alternative healthcare options, such as chiropractic care or yoga, can support your body's natural healing capabilities and contribute to overall well-being during postpartum recovery. Incorporating anti-inflammatory foods into your diet can also help reduce inflammation and accelerate your recovery.

Naturally, as a place of refuge, your home becomes an essential haven for comfort measures. Pillows, more than mere sleep accessories, become supportive tools strategically positioned to facilitate optimal breastfeeding or arranged to ease back pain. The ambiance of your room, adjusted to a soothing temperature and softened with dim lighting, promotes relaxation and supports your body's natural healing processes. Adding essential oils into the air enhances this environment; scents like lavender, known for its calming properties, and peppermint, which energizes the spirit, act as subtle supporters for your recovery. It's important to consult your health care provider about the use of essential oils in the presence of babies under three years old. It's possible that you may want to incorporate these oils in your bathing rituals or when you are in another room while baby naps. These elements can work together to enhance your home's nurturing and healing atmosphere. Natural approaches are all about giving you a holistic way to manage pain and discomfort during the post-partum period, making your recovery a bit more comfortable and peaceful.

While many prefer natural methods for alleviating discomfort, it's crucial to recognize when professional intervention is necessary. Pain that intensifies rather than subsides, or discomfort accompanied by fever, may signal complications such as infection. Similarly, breastfeeding challenges that cause severe pain or significantly impede the process should prompt a consultation with a lactation specialist to ensure both mother and baby are supported. Recognizing these signs is vital in distinguishing between average recovery experiences and potential concerns, guiding mothers to seek the expertise and reassurance of health-care professionals when needed. This vigilant approach ensures that postpartum recovery is manageable and safe, prioritizing the health and well-being of both mother and child.

EMBRACING REST DAYS

Rest days are essential to the postpartum recovery process. These aren't merely brief pauses but vital opportunities that promote physical healing and mental peace. After childbirth, both body and mind adapt to significant changes and challenges. Rest is more than a physical necessity during this time—it becomes a critical component of holistic recovery. Taking time to rest helps in regaining strength and processing the intense experiences of childbirth, allowing new mothers to rejuvenate and reconnect with themselves as they navigate the new realities of motherhood.

Creating an environment conducive to rest involves more than selecting comfortable pillows or cozy bedding; it's about designing a sanctuary that supports undisturbed sleep. Installing blackout curtains can mimic the deep tranquility of night, while white noise machines mask disruptive sounds from the outside world. Introducing the gentle scent of lavender, known for its calming properties, can further enhance the atmosphere and promote deeper sleep.

The advice to "sleep when the baby sleeps" is a common refrain in parenting circles, often easier said than done. The challenge arises when daytime responsibilities accumulate, competing fiercely for a mother's attention. A deliberate shift in priorities is necessary to embrace this wisdom, placing the mother's rest at the forefront as an essential, non-negotiable element of her day. This may mean accepting a less-than-spotless home or leaning on the support of others through delegation. While these adjustments may require embracing some imperfection, the benefits of a sharper mind and a more resilient body are worth following through for.

Restful periods are not just about pausing the physical hustle but an opportunity to engage in activities that rejuvenate the spirit and fortify the bond with your newborn. Imagine those precious moments of cuddling with your baby, where time slows down, and the world shrinks to just the warm, peaceful cocoon of your embrace.

How about some quiet time with baby-friendly tunes? Soft music can soothe your nerves and those of your little one. Or try a gentle massage for your baby, turning a simple routine into an enriching bonding session that leaves both of you more relaxed. You could also take a leisurely walk with the stroller; fresh air is invigorating and a sensory feast for your baby.

Additionally, consider setting up a mini reading nook. Snuggling up with a colorful picture book can create cherished memories. Another lovely activity is baby yoga, a delightful way to stretch and strengthen your body while your baby joins in with simple movements. While gentle on the body, these activities profoundly nourish the soul, intertwining rest, tranquility, and playfulness into your daily rhythm and creating an enriching bonding experience for you and your little one.

ENERGY UPDATE

As you navigate this journey of rest and recovery, it's essential to differentiate between activities that uplift and those that deplete your energy level. Take a moment to sit back and reflect. List the activities that feed your spirit versus those that drain you. This introspection helps cultivate a deeper understanding of your needs and preferences, empowering you as a mother to make choices that support your recovery and enhance your overall journey through motherhood.

Consider rest not as a luxury but as a necessary healing embrace for both your body and soul. As you navigate the postpartum period, try to create a calming oasis for yourself, making the most of those precious moments to sleep, choosing activities that rejuvenate you, and understanding what truly refuels your energy. This foundational pillar of rest, enriched with the knowledge and strategies we've explored together, sets the stage for a recovery that nurtures your physical health and helps to deepen the bond between yourself and your baby. As you move forward, let the wisdom of rest guide you, strengthening you for the beautiful, ongoing adventure of parenthood with resilience and joy.

During the postpartum period, your body communicates in subtle ways, signaling its needs through gentle whispers. If you listen carefully, these cues can guide you wisely through recovery. The signals range from the unmistakable, such as profound fatigue following a night of interrupted sleep, to more subtle indications, like mood shifts that might hint at a need for some quiet time alone or the rejuvenating company of friends. Recognizing these cues requires mindfulness that grows with daily practice. This attentiveness helps you align with your body's rhythms and needs, supporting the recovery process.

Imagine a typical afternoon when deep weariness sets in—not just a longing for sleep, but a fatigue that casts a shadow of overwhelm across everything. This experience, all too familiar for new moms, is your body sending an SOS for rest. Answering this call may mean tucking your baby into a snug, safe nook for a few peaceful moments, taking a deep breath, and allowing your body to unwind, even if sleep remains elusive. This simple act of heeding and responding can pivot the direction of your day, bringing a sense of renewal that nurtures both you and your baby.

In the quiet moments scattered throughout the day, opportunities to reflect often emerge—a gentle, inward exploration of life's complexities. During these pauses, the approach to self-care, initially pursued with determination and careful planning, calls for a thoughtful review. Finding the right balance isn't about adhering to a strict plan; it's about navigating each day with flexible adaptability and adjusting to life's shifting needs, desires, and circumstances. Thus, revisiting self-care goals becomes a ritual of recalibration, ensuring you are in harmony with the ever-changing rhythms of life.

NOURISHING YOUR BODY FOR ENERGY AND HEALING

During the early months of motherhood, when sleep is scarce and hormones fluctuate, nourishing yourself transcends mere eating; it becomes a critical strategy for restoring energy and achieving emotional stability. Foods rich in vitamins, minerals, and essential fatty acids are vital allies in nutrition. For instance, with their complex carbohydrates, oats offer a sustained release of energy, helping to mitigate the abrupt energy spikes and crashes associated with simpler sugars. When paired with omega-3-rich chia seeds, this nutritious combination maintains steady energy levels and supports brain health, which is crucial for navigating the challenges of sleep deprivation and new parenting responsibilities.

Leafy greens such as spinach and kale are nutritional power-houses, rich in iron, folic acid, and B vitamins, essential for fighting fatigue and stabilizing mood. These nutrients are especially important as they help combat the iron deficiency many new mothers experience postpartum. Additionally, incorporating protein-rich foods like eggs and legumes into daily meals is vital for bodily repair and strength. Proteins also play a role in stabilizing blood sugar levels, helping to manage the erratic hunger pangs common among new mothers.

Moreover, though often overlooked, water plays a key role during the postpartum period, affecting every aspect of your recovery and breastfeeding. Adequate hydration facilitates the body's healing processes and is vital for milk production, supporting breastfeeding mothers in meeting their infants' nutritional needs. Additionally, staying hydrated helps regulate body temperature, which can be particularly helpful for mothers with postpartum night sweats. Including beverages like herbal teas can offer further benefits, such as improving digestion and providing moments of relaxation in the hectic routine of caring for a newborn. These teas boost your body's moisture level and create soothing rituals that bring a sense of tranquility to a new mother's day. However, keep in mind that while breastfeeding, some herbal teas have the potential to affect your milk supply, stimulate the uterus, cause allergic reactions, or have other adverse effects. It is important to speak with your healthcare provider before consuming any herbal products.

As you find comfort in these small rituals, remember that smart snacking is also important for maintaining your energy and overall health. Carefully chosen snacks can deliver quick, concentrated bursts of nutrition without the time commitment required for full meals. Almonds and walnuts, loaded with healthy fats and protein, are ideal for snacking during the short breaks between feedings, providing an instant energy boost. Apple slices paired with almond butter create a delightful mix of sweet and savory, blending the fruit's natural sugars with the sustained energy from fats and proteins. For those moments when a little indulgence is needed, dark chocolate can be a guilt-free treat due to its antioxidant properties and mood-enhancing effects, nourishing both body and spirit.

As a new mom in today's fast-paced world, every minute of your day is precious. Handy kitchen appliances can be a real lifesaver, helping you balance nutrition with the need for convenience. Consider the slow cooker, for example—it's a lifesaver. You can toss in the ingredients, set it, and forget it. A warm, nourishing meal is ready when dinner rolls around, and no fuss is required. And for those days when even spooning food onto a plate seems like a task, there's the blender. It's perfect for blending quick, nutrient-packed smoothies with your favorite fruits, veggies, and protein powder, giving you a healthy meal in minutes.

Then there's the Instant Pot, which is incredibly versatile. Whether you're sautéing veggies or cooking a stew, it cuts down the time you spend cooking without compromising the variety or healthiness of your meals. These appliances simplify your cooking process, so you can spend less time in the kitchen and more time enjoying your new little one, all while keeping healthy eating on track.

Quick Meal Options

In the spirit of practicality and nourishment, the following meal ideas are designed to fuel new mothers with minimal time investment. These suggestions cater to both traditional and vegan dietary preferences, ensuring every mother can find energy and healing. These meal ideas are straightforward yet nutritious, helping mothers maintain their energy and health without spending too much time in the kitchen.

1. Greek yogurt mixed with honey and topped with walnuts, perfect for a quick breakfast or a refreshing snack.
2. Scrambled eggs combined with spinach and feta cheese offer a hearty start to the day.
3. Quinoa salad tossed with black beans, corn, and avocado is a light yet filling meal.
4. Turkey and avocado wrap using a whole-grain tortilla is ideal for a quick lunch.
5. Lentil soup served with whole-grain bread is comforting and nutritious.
6. Chicken stir-fry with a variety of vegetables is a versatile dinner option.
7. Salmon served with roasted sweet potatoes and steamed broccoli, a balanced and satisfying meal.

8. Beef and vegetable stew is perfect for preparing ahead and reheating.
9. Pasta with tomato sauce and lean ground beef is a classic dish that's always a hit.
10. Tuna salad on whole-grain bread is great for a no-fuss lunch.

Quick Vegan Options

1. Avocado toast on whole grain bread topped with radish slices and a sprinkle of sesame seeds, quick and fulfilling.
2. Smoothie bowl with blended bananas, spinach, and almond milk, topped with sliced almonds and berries.
3. Chickpea salad with cucumbers, tomatoes, and a lemon-tahini dressing is great for a refreshing lunch.
4. Vegan wraps filled with hummus, grated carrots, and mixed greens wrapped in a whole wheat tortilla.
5. Lentil soup with carrots, celery, and spices, served with a side of toasted pita bread.
6. Stir-fried tofu with bell peppers, broccoli, and soy sauce served over brown rice.
7. Stuffed sweet potatoes with black beans, corn, and a dollop of guacamole, hearty and satisfying.
8. Pasta salad with cherry tomatoes, olives, cucumber, and a balsamic vinaigrette.
9. Vegetable curry with coconut milk served over jasmine rice is rich in flavors and comforting.
10. BBQ tempeh sandwich with coleslaw on whole grain bread, perfect for a quick dinner.

Sample Meal Plan

Breakfast:

- Avocado toast with poached eggs
- Chia pudding with mixed berries and coconut flakes
- Scrambled eggs with spinach and feta cheese
- Overnight oats with almond butter and sliced banana
- Whole grain pancakes with maple syrup and sliced strawberries
- Veggie omelet with whole-grain toast
- Smoothie bowl with spinach, banana, and almond milk topped with nuts and seeds

Lunch:

- Quinoa salad with roasted vegetables and feta cheese
- Sweet potato and black bean chili
- Split pea soup with whole-grain bread
- Grilled chicken Caesar salad
- Veggie stir-fry with tofu and brown rice
- Caprese salad with fresh mozzarella, tomatoes, and basil
- Chickpea salad with cucumber, tomato, and lemon-tahini dressing

Dinner:

- Baked salmon with roasted sweet potatoes and asparagus
- Spaghetti with marinara sauce and garlic bread
- Grilled steak with mashed potatoes and green beans
- Vegetarian chili with cornbread
- Teriyaki chicken stir-fry with bell peppers and rice noodles

- Homemade pizza with whole wheat crust and assorted toppings
- Roast chicken with quinoa pilaf and steamed broccoli

Snacks:

- Hummus and veggie sticks
- Apple slices with almond or peanut butter
- Trail mix with nuts and dried fruit
- Pumpkin seeds and dried cranberries
- Rice cakes with avocado and tomato slices

Desserts:

- Dark chocolate and nut clusters
- Frozen yogurt bark
- Mixed berry fruit salad with mint

Having a meal plan helps eliminate the guesswork about what to eat, ensuring that both mom and baby are well-fed and nourished throughout the week!

As we wrap up this deep dive into the postpartum period, let's remember that recovery is not just about physical healing; it's a comprehensive journey that includes emotional and spiritual healing. Navigating this transformative phase with care and patience, using traditional and creative approaches to comfort and health, can significantly enhance your recovery. By embracing a mix of rest, nourishment, and gentle activity, you're setting yourself up for a more balanced and joyful motherhood experience. It's all about finding what works best for you and your body as you adjust to this new chapter in life, allowing you to thrive as a mother and a vibrant individual.

CHAPTER FOUR

INCORPORATING WELLNESS PRACTICES AT HOME

Adjusting expectations around fitness and activity levels isn't about lowering your standards but tuning them to your current reality. Your body, in its post-birth recovery phase, operates at a different rhythm and has different needs than before pregnancy. Embracing this reality fosters a gentler internal dialogue—one that celebrates every bit of progress and views recovery as a journey, not a sprint. This approach not only encourages patience but also helps cultivate a sense of accomplishment and peace with your body's natural healing process.

For example, opting for a gentle morning activity, like a stroll in the park with the stroller, can refresh both body and mind, setting you up beautifully for the day ahead. On the flip side, sensing a need for rest could mean turning down an invitation and choosing to spend a tranquil day at home instead. This interplay between activity and rest, steered by your body's signals, fosters holistic recovery and cultivates patience and self-compassion.

MOVEMENT AND EXERCISE

Starting a conversation with your postpartum body about when to resume physical activity calls for a considerate and respectful approach, recognizing the unique pace of healing and adaptation your body sets. This dialogue often starts with introducing gentle movements—a thoughtful, gentle re-entry into the world of exercise that respects your body's recent journey and its current state of recovery. These gentle movements help bridge the gap back to more robust activities and reaffirm your body's abilities and resilience. Simple exercises like pelvic tilts and wall push-ups, though modest in exertion, play a crucial role in reactivating muscle memory and rebuilding your connection with your physical self.

Listening to your body's feedback as you begin postpartum exercise transforms the experience into a two-way conversation rather than a one-sided directive. This careful attention helps you distinguish between the natural feelings of reactivating dormant muscles and the warning signs of distress or overexertion, which might require you to pause or modify your activities. This nuanced understanding is critical—it recognizes the thin line between beneficial discomfort, a signal of growth and strengthening, and actual pain, which clearly advises you to stop and reassess. For instance, a gentle stretch that awakens the muscles in your lower back may bring a welcome sense of relief, while a sharp pain during that same movement would be a clear signal to stop immediately and possibly seek advice.

Gradually elevating your fitness routine while focusing on continuous improvement and adaptation reflects the evolving nature of postpartum recovery itself. This approach encourages progressively challenging yourself, setting realistic goals that adapt as your body regains strength and stamina. Initially, these goals may focus on consistency, like incorporating gentle movements into your daily routine, and later shift toward enhancing strength or flexibility. Tracking your progress, whether through journaling or digital apps, not only motivates but also provides concrete proof of the empowering journey your body is undertaking as it reclaims its capabilities.

The advantages of reintegrating exercise into your daily routine extend well beyond physical benefits, profoundly influencing your mental and emotional health. Engaging in gentle exercises like stretching, which focuses on flexibility and controlled breathing, not only engages your muscles but also promotes relaxation—perfect for counterbalancing the physical demands of childcare. Additionally, low-impact activities such as swimming or cycling on a stationary bike enhance cardiovascular fitness without over-burdening your joints or pelvic floor. These activities release endorphins that naturally boost your mood, helping to clear the haze of sleep deprivation and stabilize the emotional ups and downs often experienced postpartum.

Setting and achieving even modest fitness goals during this time can instill a sense of accomplishment and confidence, reinforcing the value of physical activity not just for bodily recovery but as a vital self-care practice that enriches your journey toward overall wellness. Choose these activities based on your body's current condition and personal preferences to seamlessly integrate movement into your postpartum recovery.

As you return to physical activity after childbirth, the journey is one of patience, attentiveness, and gradual progression. It's a path that honors your body's recent experience, recognizes its current state, and looks forward to its future strength. You can effectively support your recovery by engaging in gentle movements, tuning into your body's signals, setting realistic goals, and appreciating the comprehensive benefits of exercise. Thus, reintegrating movement and exercise into the postpartum period becomes a holistic act of self-care, affirming both your body's capabilities and your spirit's resilience.

WALKING: THE UNDERRATED EXERCISE

Walking is a wonderfully simple yet effective part of postnatal recovery, blending physical healing, mental refreshment, and emotional balance. This easy form of exercise does a lot more than just get you moving. The steady rhythm of walking, in sync with your breathing, turns a basic activity into a nurturing practice for your body, a calming moment for your mind, and a lift for your spirit. It's a straightforward way to feel better all around.

Integrating walking into your daily life shouldn't feel like a chore; the aim is for it to become a natural part of your routine, enhancing well-being without adding stress. How walking fits into a new mother's life can vary, with each method tailored to her unique circumstances. For instance, a walk with the stroller offers multiple advantages—it provides the gentle rocking that often calms a fussy baby and gives the mother a change of scenery and fresh air. Evening walks with the family foster bonds through shared experiences, creating precious moments of connection that can be missed in the daily rush. For those motivated by measurable progress, a step tracker can help set realistic, incremental goals, encouraging movement without the pressure to perform.

During these walks, paying close attention to what your body tells you is substantial. It's a conversation between what you can do and what you hope to achieve. Begin slowly by respecting your body's current pace, recognizing the hard work done through childbirth and its ongoing recovery. Gradually increasing the distance and intensity shows you're listening carefully, tuning into the signs that you're ready for more or perhaps need a break. This careful approach makes sure that walking boosts your energy rather than draining it, keeping the activity in line with your body's needs and helping it regain full strength.

Walking does more than benefit the body—it also enhances social and emotional well-being. For a new mom, taking walks with her baby helps build a close bond, turning each outing into an adventure of exploration and discovery. The smooth rhythm and sway of the stroller can foster connection, offering precious, undistracted time with your child. Additionally, walking with other new moms can forge a supportive community, a place for sharing experiences and challenges with understanding and encouragement. This social side of walking turns it into a shared journey through motherhood, enriching it with an emotional depth that goes well beyond simple physical activity.

Walking with your baby opens up a world of sensory experiences, whether you're meandering through peaceful nature trails or lively urban parks. Nature walks bring the calming presence of green spaces, offering a quiet beauty that can relax the mind and lift spirits. The variety of landscapes, the sounds of nature, and the ever-changing seasons create a serene environment where both mom and baby can enjoy moments of peace and happiness. On the other hand, urban walks provide a stimulating view of diverse people, striking architecture, and bustling activity, sparking curiosity and introducing both mother and child to the community's vibrant life. These different settings add a flexible and enriching activity for moms and babies, opening doors to new experiences that promote growth, learning, and connection.

SETTING WELLNESS GOALS

Setting wellness goals is a powerful way to show commitment to health and vitality in managing both self-care and motherhood. These goals serve as checkpoints, marking the path to a balanced lifestyle where enjoying physical activity becomes not just a hope but a daily reality. Identifying and embracing these goals involves a thoughtful exploration of personal preferences and possibilities. Discovering what truly brings joy and revitalizes the spirit is necessary to maintain regular involvement and find fulfillment in the routine of physical self-care.

Make exercise a treasured part of your daily life, not just a chore. Finding activities that resonate with you is key to creating a lasting wellness routine, especially during the postpartum period. Consider this search a personal journey to discover what truly moves you, almost like finding a melody that stirs your soul. For some, the rhythmic beat of dance isn't just a workout but a celebration of freedom and joy. For others, the soothing calm of swimming provides both a physical workout and mental relaxation. Choosing the suitable activity isn't about sticking to strict programs; it's about listening to your body's cues and desires for expression through movement, ensuring that exercise becomes a treasured part of your daily life rather than another heavy commitment.

In the postpartum period, it's crucial to consider your current physical condition and everyday lifestyle needs. Choose activities that align with your body's readiness and limitations, knowing that they can be adapted to different stages of recovery. For example, water aerobics is a fantastic option because the buoyancy of the water supports your body, reducing strain while still offering resistance—perfect for gently easing back into exercise. Pilates is also ideal as it focuses on core strength and flexibility and can be adapted to different stages of recovery, providing a supportive way to build your physical resilience. As you look for ways to integrate wellness into your new routine, consider involving your baby in your exercise activities.

Bringing your baby into your exercise routines is a creative way to manage self-care while juggling the responsibilities of motherhood. This approach helps you stay active and provides a special bonding experience with your little one. This blend of caregiving and fitness eliminates obstacles to staying active, turning workout sessions into opportunities for fun. For example, baby yoga can spark laughter and strengthen connections, making physical activity a playful time together. You can also try baby-wearing dance, which allows you to move to the music with your baby securely strapped to you. This provides an excellent rhythmic workout and soothes and entertains your baby with the movement and music. Another great option is to engage in aquatic activities like "mommy and me" swim classes, which are fantastic for both mother and baby. These classes help babies get comfortable in the water at an early age and provide moms with a gentle, supportive way to exercise. These activities promote physical health and enhance the emotional connection between mother and child, weaving wellness naturally into daily family life.

Introducing fitness into family life can start early, even for new parents with just one baby. Attaching a baby trailer to your bicycle transforms a regular ride into a fun adventure, allowing you to safely share the joys of the outdoors with your baby. You can also tailor gentle hikes to accommodate carrying your baby, whether in a carrier or a stroller, making it an excellent way for both of you to get fresh air and experience nature together. These activities are perfect for new parents looking to incorporate health and wellness into their family's routine right from the start, teaching the value of physical activity through enjoyable and shared experiences.

Within your ever-changing family life, where each day brings new rhythms and challenges, setting and pursuing wellness goals becomes a vibrant, ongoing journey. This process respects the body's recovery, celebrates the pleasure of movement, and strengthens connections that enhance both personal and family life. By intentionally exploring what works best for them and aligning activities with individual and family needs, new mothers can shape a wellness path that supports their recovery, rejuvenates their spirit, and exemplifies a healthy, vibrant lifestyle for their family.

The true value of setting wellness goals is not achieving perfection but striving for balance, joy, and fulfillment. This goal-setting strategy recognizes the unique experiences of each mother, providing insight and tools that support both personal and family wellness. Moving forward, let this commitment to intentional wellness inspire ongoing growth and a deeper appreciation for the beautiful journey of motherhood.

SEEKING PROFESSIONAL GUIDANCE

Navigating postpartum recovery involves more than just personal effort; it often requires a supportive community, including emotional support and professional guidance. Healthcare providers and fitness experts who specialize in postpartum care become invaluable allies for new mothers. They guide you through recovery with their expertise and empathy, ensuring you have the knowledge and support needed to heal and thrive.

Setting up a consultation to discuss postpartum fitness plans or any concerns regarding recovery can shed light on the best way forward, providing reassurance and personalized advice. This proactive and informed step ensures that the path back to wellness is effective and safe, respecting the body's pace and acknowledging the unique experiences of each new mother.

Incorporating wellness goals and fitness routines into your life as a new mom isn't just about regaining strength or reshaping your body; it's about nurturing your well-being and creating moments of self-care that rejuvenate your spirit. As you adjust to motherhood, consider integrating gentle, realistic fitness activities that fit seamlessly into your new routine, whether a yoga session during naptime or a brisk walk with the stroller. Remember, these activities are not just physical exercises but vital practices that help maintain your mental and emotional health, giving you the endurance and positivity needed to enjoy this beautiful, transformative time. Embrace these practices not as another task on your to-do list but as cherished, empowering moments for yourself, celebrating each step as a milestone toward a balanced and joyful life.

CHAPTER FIVE

THE EMOTIONAL LANDSCAPE OF NEW MOTHERHOOD

The emotional landscape for a new mother during the postpartum period can feel like sailing a vast ocean under a moonlit sky—gorgeous but unpredictable, calm yet quickly shifting to stormy. Here, many new moms encounter what's known as the baby blues, a brief period of emotional turmoil. While it's a common experience, it's important to distinguish the baby blues from more serious conditions like postpartum depression, as they are often mistaken for one another but require different approaches.

THE BABY BLUES

The baby blues, a topic often quietly mentioned in maternity wards and at baby showers, is a temporary phase of emotional sensitivity and mood swings that many new mothers go through after giving birth. The baby blues, affecting about 70–80 percent of new moms, are less severe and shorter in duration compared to more intense conditions like postpartum depression. Mothers must understand this difference, as it helps them recognize and manage their feelings confidently, alleviating undue worry.

Symptoms of baby blues can include sudden bouts of crying, feelings of sadness or emptiness, irritability, and unexpected mood swings. These emotional fluctuations typically begin a few days after delivery and usually resolve within two weeks. While challenging, this period of emotional upheaval is a normal response as the body adjusts hormonally and emotionally to the changes post-birth. It's essential for new mothers to understand that these feelings are both common and temporary. Support from family, friends, and healthcare professionals can play a crucial role in navigating these early days, helping to assure mothers that they are not alone and that help is available as they adjust to their new role.

The baby blues are primarily influenced by a dramatic shift in hormonal levels that occurs after childbirth, particularly the rapid decrease in hormones like estrogen and progesterone. These hormones rise significantly during pregnancy and drop sharply following delivery, disrupting the body's chemical balance. The stress hormone cortisol may also fluctuate during this period, further impacting emotional stability. This hormonal upheaval, combined with physical exhaustion from childbirth and the immediate demands of newborn care, creates a perfect storm for emotional shifts. Understanding these scientific and biological foundations helps frame the baby blues as a natural response to these physiological changes, reassuring new mothers that these feelings are common and typically short-lived.

RECOGNIZING SIGNS OF POSTPARTUM DEPRESSION (PPD)

It's important to distinguish between the short-lived baby blues and the more profound, more persistent signs of postpartum depression (PPD). Understanding this difference is pertinent—not just in how intense or long-lasting the symptoms are, but in how they affect daily life. PPD can make it challenging for a mom to connect with her baby, manage everyday tasks, or enjoy activities she used to love. Signs like ongoing sadness, severe mood swings, or pulling back from friends and family mean it may be time to reach out for professional help. This distinction often relies on carefully observing one's emotional state and how well one can function daily. Symptoms that last beyond two weeks, like continuous sadness that affects all aspects of life, losing joy in favorite activities, or overwhelming fear that prevents caring for oneself or the baby indicate that these feelings may be more than just the baby blues. Recognizing these symptoms is the first step toward healing, and although intimidating, it is the first step toward regaining emotional balance.

Alongside postpartum depression (PPD) is the often-overlooked path of postpartum anxiety, a condition that, while related to depression, stands out with its own set of challenges. Postpartum anxiety presents with intense worry or fear that makes everyday tasks feel overwhelming. This kind of anxiety can fill a mother's mind with constant concerns about her baby's health, her skills as a parent, or other worries—some realistic, some not. Symptoms like heart palpitations, trouble sleeping, and restlessness are signs that this anxiety is more than just the usual new mom nerves; it's something that needs recognition and proper care, highlighting the importance of understanding it as distinct from the more widely recognized postpartum depression.

The risk of developing postpartum depression (PPD) and post-partum anxiety doesn't reflect a mother's strength or her readiness for motherhood. Instead, it often results from a mix of risk factors that increase their likelihood. Factors such as a history of mental health challenges, lack of support, complications during childbirth, and the intense sleep deprivation that comes with caring for a newborn all play a role. Understanding these risk factors isn't about predicting a particular outcome but about encouraging awareness and proactive measures. This approach emphasizes the importance of prevention and timely intervention, which can help lessen the severity and duration of these conditions.

Let's paint a picture with a couple of real-life stories because, trust me, you're not the only one going through this.

Meet Tatum. She's a new mom, just like you. But lately, she's been feeling like she's stuck in a fog of sadness and anxiety. She loves her baby to bits, but an overwhelming sense of guilt creeps in because she struggles to connect. Sleep? Forget about it—she's exhausted but can't seem to catch a break. And those friends and family she used to hang out with? She's been keeping her distance lately, feeling ashamed of not feeling the happiness she expected.

Then there's Abigail. She's on a rollercoaster ride of emotions. She's snapping at everyone one minute, and the next, she's drowning in tears. Handling even the simplest tasks feels like climbing Mount Everest, and she's losing interest in things she used to love. Inside, she's falling apart, but on the outside, she's putting on a brave face because that's what you're supposed to do, right?

Now, here's the thing—if you're nodding along to any of this, it's okay. Seriously. You're not alone, and you're not failing as a mom. PPD can hit anyone, and it's nothing to be ashamed of.

RECOGNIZING OVERWHELM

As a new mom, it can feel like you're caught in a whirlwind of responsibilities, expectations, and pure exhaustion. When everything feels overwhelming and urgent, these moments call for recognition and practical strategies to find a more transparent, calmer outlook. Start by setting small, achievable daily goals to give yourself a sense of accomplishment and structure. Establishing a routine for you and your baby can bring comfort and predictability to your day, reducing stress and boosting overall well-being. However, the first step in dealing with these overwhelming demands is recognizing the early signs of stress. Physically, you may notice a tight chest, a racing heart, shallow breathing, headaches, muscle tension, and fatigue. Emotionally, you might feel irritable, dread the day ahead, or have a strong urge to withdraw from everything, accompanied by sadness, helplessness, and even anger. Acknowledging these signs as genuine indicators of distress rather than flaws or failures is crucial. It's okay to feel this way; recognizing these feelings is the first step toward finding balance again.

Practical coping strategies can significantly ease your stress once you recognize that you're feeling overwhelmed. Mindfulness, which involves staying fully present in the moment without judgment, is a particularly effective tool. It can be as simple as paying attention to your breath as it moves in and out, helping to ground you when you feel like you're on the edge. Techniques for prioritizing tasks can also help by allowing you to sort through the many demands vying for your attention. By focusing on what needs immediate attention and setting aside less urgent tasks, you can alleviate the pressure that contributes to overwhelm. Recall your Yes/No! Worksheet. Start a checklist now. Or go through the mental clutter and deliberately push away what is not your immediate priority. Clearing the space and returning to center can be achievable in just a few minutes. This approach helps clear the fog of stress, making it easier to manage your responsibilities one step at a time.

Setting realistic expectations for yourself and your family is central to balancing the expected and the unexpected. Balance may include reconsidering what your definition of a successful day looks like. Recognizing that success in new motherhood isn't measured by completing a to-do list but by the care you provide to yourself and your child. Success can be found in the joy of shared laughter during meals, the comfort of a warm hug, and the peace in brief rest moments. Grounding your expectations in the realities of everyday life rather than in a perfect ideal helps shield against overwhelm, allowing for a manageable and deeply fulfilling lifestyle. Remember, completing just one task or taking five minutes for yourself is a triumph. Success can be found through contentment and meaning in the smallest of moments.

Our culture has us believing that asking for help is often seen as a sign of defeat, wrapped in undue shame. Yet, the reality is quite the opposite. Recognizing the need for support and actively seeking it out shows strength, not weakness. Partners, family, friends, and professionals all share in the experience. Whether asking a relative to watch the baby for a bit, consulting a therapist, or simply venting to a friend, each step to reach out builds a more robust support network, ensuring you're not facing challenges alone when they arise.

OVERCOMING MOM GUILT

Amid new motherhood, where every decision feels like a big deal, mom guilt tends to sneak in and steal our joy from those little wins. It's like this nagging feeling that we're not measuring up, fueled by societal pressures, personal expectations, and those picture-perfect lives we see on social media. But guess what? Recognizing that mom guilt is just a mash-up of outside pressures and our own worries is the first step to shaking it off and reclaiming our confidence and happiness.

Mom guilt usually springs from the usual suspects—feeling like we're not nailing this whole parenting thing, struggling to balance work and home life, or worrying about giving enough attention and care to our new baby. These feelings can mess with our emotional well-being, cranking up the stress, tanking our self-esteem, and clouding those moments of connection and joy with unnecessary fretting. But knowing these triggers and their oversized impact is the first move in taking back control and reshaping those guilt-inducing stories that love to camp out in our heads.

So, how do we tackle those guilt-tripping thoughts? It's all about flipping the script from self-criticism to understanding and acceptance. Start by catching those guilt-tripping thoughts when they pop up, then hit pause and question where they're coming from and if they're even true. Most of the time, they're born from unrealistic expectations we've set for ourselves or soaked up from the world around us rather than actual slip-ups or failures. By consciously shifting our perspective—recognizing the effort we're putting in, the hurdles we're clearing, and the messy beauty of motherhood—we can start to loosen guilt's grip and replace it with a kinder, more realistic view of ourselves and our journey.

And don't underestimate the power of self-compassion exercises. Talking to yourself as you would to a dear friend or repeating affirmations that celebrate your efforts and intentions—simple stuff like this can work wonders for dialing down that mom guilt. Make them part of your daily routine, and they become gentle reminders of your worth, hustle, and motherhood's glorious chaos. Over time, they create a mental space less hospitable to guilt, leaving you more at peace with the parenting rollercoaster.

When mom guilt's got you feeling heavy, don't be afraid to lean on your tribe. Opening up to close pals, family, or support groups about those feelings of guilt and inadequacy lightens the load and shows how moms face these struggles every day. Sharing experiences builds a sense of community and comfort, softening guilt's blow with the warmth of shared understanding and encouragement. Embracing vulnerability and seeking support can not only alleviate the weight of mom guilt but also foster self-compassion and resilience, strengthened by the shared experiences and empathy of your tribe.

Lastly, try writing down your guilt trip in detail. After you are done, read it entirely and immediately shift your attention to what your body feels like. Feel the weight of this trip. Define its edges and boundaries. What color is it? What is its texture? Feel the road under this guilt trip and notice where it goes. Then, take your pen and put a big, fat X across the entire page. Take a deep breath in, and on a loud and forceful exhale, take that guilt trip and blow it out of your body like the winds from a hurricane. If you feel any remnants, blow it out again! Mentally remove it and make space in your body for fresh air. Notice how much more clearly you think now that the energy has shifted. Take a deep breath in, filling it with compassion and self-love, and on the exhale, simply repeat your strongest and most favorite affirmation. If you don't have a personalized affirmation, you can lovingly say, "These ideas do not serve my best self. I don't have time for them. You can leave now."

Conclude with "What little act of kindness can I show myself right now?" As you write down your thoughts or mentally recognize them, ponder how you can treat yourself with gentleness and understanding. This simple reflection and intention-setting set the stage for a future filled with growth, resilience, and heaps of self-love.

HANDLING EMOTIONAL UPS AND DOWNS

While navigating postpartum depression and anxiety, finding any positives might seem tricky. However, during these challenging times, many moms discover a deep well of resilience and inner strength. This exercise invites you to reflect on the challenges you're facing and the bright spots and growth accompanying them. It's a great way to acknowledge and celebrate small victories as you move through this complex time. You can also talk through these prompts aloud. Speaking your thoughts can be just as powerful as writing them down. The goal is to help you clear out those heavy emotions, relieve yourself of their weight, and shift the energy to make more room for you.

- Can you recall a hard day you had after your baby arrived? What were you feeling?
- What's something you've learned about yourself as a mom through these challenges?
- Who has helped you out a lot during this postpartum period? What did their help show you about friendship and support?

- During one of those tough days, did anything positive surprise you? What was it?
- What's one thing you've learned from your experiences that you want to remember as a parent?
- Who loves you?
- Who do you love?

This exercise is about recognizing how tough things can be and how much you can grow and become stronger. It's about understanding that even though postpartum depression and anxiety can bring a lot of pain and fear, there's also a chance for healing. Support from others can make a big difference, and a special, lasting connection between you and your child can develop from these experiences.

New motherhood can feel overwhelming, but incorporating self-help strategies into your daily routine can provide moments of stability and much-needed respite. Engaging in physical activity, whether a calming walk or a gentle yoga session, can soothe your body and mind, easing built-up tensions. Practices like journaling, guided meditation, and listening to music offer avenues for emotional release and relaxation. Open communication with others helps reinforce the understanding that these feelings are shared and valid and that no mother is alone in her experiences. Maintaining a regular rest schedule and staying mindful, focusing on being present and accepting, can highlight moments of joy and foster a sense of peace. Prioritizing self-care through simple acts of kindness, like indulging in a warm bath or savoring a favorite snack, offers immediate comfort. And remember to incorporate attention exercises throughout your day to keep you centered and grounded. Engaging in these practices can provide significant emotional support and contribute to a smoother transition through this challenging phase. Remember that it's okay to prioritize your well-being and that self-care is not selfish. It's not Me First. It's Me Too.

BREAKING THE STIGMA

Conversations about mental health, particularly when it comes to motherhood, are frequently cloaked in silence, hiding how common and normal these issues truly are. By openly discussing postpartum depression and anxiety, whether with close friends or on public platforms, we can break through this silence. This shift turns private struggles into shared stories, breaking down the stigma that can isolate and overwhelm individuals. Such conversations connect people to a community that offers support, understanding, and collective strength. I get it if you're feeling shy or embarrassed to ask for help. But remember, there's strength in seeking support. Here's how you can start.

1. **Normalize your feelings**. Talk about it. Share your struggles with friends or join online communities where you'll find other moms who've been there and done that.
2. **Accept practical help**. Let someone watch the baby for a bit so you can catch your breath or ask for a hand with household chores. You'd be surprised how much a little help can lift your spirits.
3. **Reach out for professional support**. Therapy's on the table. It's not a sign of weakness—it's a way to take control of your mental health. But where do you start? You can start with your OB-GYN or primary care physician; they can connect you with mental health resources or refer you to a therapist specializing in postpartum care. Additionally, online directories like

Psychology Today (psychologytoday.com/us) or
TherapyDen (www.therapyden.com) allow you to search
for therapists in your area based on specialty and
insurance coverage. Postpartum Support International
(www.postpartum.net) offers resources and a helpline
specifically for moms struggling with perinatal mood and
anxiety disorders, including postpartum depression. If
you prefer teletherapy, many therapists offer online
sessions, which can be convenient if you have limited
childcare or transportation. Lastly, look for local support
groups in your community. Connecting with other moms
who are going through similar experiences can provide
valuable support and understanding. Remember, finding
the right therapist is like finding the perfect pair of jeans
—it may take some trial and error, but finding the right
fit can make all the difference in your journey toward
healing.

4. **Stay connected**. Even when it feels like the walls are
closing in, remember that someone cares. In Chapter 9,
we'll dive into building your support network—those
rock-solid people you can lean on when you need to
catch your breath or shoot off a quick text to feel
connected. Your support network genuinely cares about
you, so don't hesitate to reach out when you need a
hand.

As we close this chapter on navigating the emotional currents of
new motherhood, remember that the journey is deeply personal
and universally shared. Each story, including yours, adds to the
collective understanding and compassion that define our experiences as mothers. While the challenges may feel daunting, the
support systems we cultivate—through conversations, professional help, and community engagement—provide strength and

grounding. As you turn the pages of your motherhood story, know you are not alone. Each step you take is a step toward greater fortitude and understanding, illuminated by the shared light of millions of mothers worldwide. Take this chapter as a reminder that your feelings are valid, support is available, and healing is not just possible but promised.

PRIORITIZING SELF-CARE FOR NEW MOMS

"Taking care of yourself doesn't mean me first, it means me too."

— *L.R. KNOST*

You picked up this book because you knew you needed self-care strategies… but be honest: Did part of you doubt that there was any reasonable way for you to fit in self-care around your responsibilities as a new mom?

As women, and as especially as mothers, we often think that any time for ourselves is selfish. But self-care is far from being synonymous with selfishness. It's how we make sure we have the energy and emotional resolve to give everything we can to our children. You could say that they need us to take care of ourselves as much as we do them.

Even if you were pretty good at integrating self-care into your routine before your baby came along, the chances are, it's been a little more difficult lately, and that's why I wrote this book: because new moms need something a little bit more specific when it comes to self-care strategies. No one knows this better than you, so I'd like to take this opportunity to ask for your help in connecting with other new moms.

By leaving a review of this book on Amazon, you'll show other women like you how they can bring back self-care – and you'll remind them why it's necessary.

Scan the QR code to leave your review on Amazon.

There are so many women out there looking for this guidance, and your review will help to make sure they find it – without the guilt!

Thank you so much for your support. There are few communities as understanding and supportive as those that grow up around motherhood; sharing strategies and advice is one of the greatest tools at our disposal.

CHAPTER SIX

MANAGING POSTPARTUM HEALTH

M anaging postpartum health encompasses both physical and emotional care. Following the birth of a baby, a mother's body experiences significant changes that need careful attention and time to heal. Physically, this can range from recovery from childbirth to adjustments in hormonal levels, which can affect everything from energy levels to physical comfort. Emotionally, the postpartum period can be a rollercoaster, with feelings of immense joy mixed with potential anxiety and mood fluctuations.

It's essential during this time to maintain a positive outlook and actively be your own hero. Taking a proactive approach to postpartum care helps you recover and enhances your ability to enjoy this new chapter with your baby. Taking time to care for your mind and body, recognizing the signs of postpartum conditions, and seeking support are vital steps. Remember, prioritizing your health is not just about getting back to "normal"—it's about nurturing yourself and ensuring you have the energy and well-being to experience the joys of motherhood to their fullest.

UNRAVELING THE MYSTERIES OF MOMMY BRAIN

"Mommy brain," often humorously referred to when new moms experience forgetfulness, is a real phenomenon that stems from a mix of intense changes occurring after childbirth. Let's take a look at why it happens—first, consider the hormonal changes that occur post-birth. Levels of estrogen and progesterone, which were high during pregnancy, plummet after giving birth, leading to a hormonal upheaval that can directly impact how sharp you feel on a day-to-day basis. It's like your brain is recalibrating itself to its new internal environment and needs a minute to adjust. This adjustment period is a natural part of the transition into motherhood, where your body and brain are getting used to a new way of being.

As you navigate these hormonal shifts, general fatigue is another significant challenge that often arises. It isn't just about feeling weary—fatigue can significantly impact your body and mind in ways you might not expect. For starters, general fatigue affects your mental clarity and memory, making it harder to keep track of details or manage complex tasks, which is challenging when you have a lot on your plate. You may also notice your mood swinging more than usual; irritability, anxiety, and even symptoms of depression can sneak up on you when you're running on empty. Your immune system doesn't fare much better without enough rest, leaving you more vulnerable to those pesky colds and other infections. There's also the risk of accidents and injuries because when you're tired, your reaction times are slower —not what you want when safety is a priority. And if that's not enough, chronic sleep deprivation can disrupt your hunger hormones, leading to increased appetite and potential weight gain.

Furthermore, your brain is now in a permanent multitasking mode, juggling many new tasks and worries, from keeping track of feeding schedules to decoding each little cry. It's no wonder some things slip through the cracks! This shift in focus and the flood of new responsibilities can crowd out the usual day-to-day details. Lastly, emotional adjustments add another layer of complexity. The joy, anxiety, and sheer overwhelm can consume a lot of your mental bandwidth, leaving less room for other information. It's like your brain has prioritized processing these new feelings over where you left your keys! Together, these elements create a perfect storm where it's easy to feel scatterbrained. This foggy phase is just that—a phase, and everyone recovers at their own pace. As you grow into your new role, clarity will return. This adjustment period is a natural part of recovery; your body is doing its best to adapt and heal.

NUTRITION FOR COGNITIVE HEALTH

Eating a variety of fruits and vegetables provides essential vitamins and minerals that are crucial not just for your brain health but for your overall well-being. Each nutrient plays a specific role in supporting mental clarity and bodily functions. Here's a look at some essential vitamins and minerals found in fruits and vegetables and how they benefit your health.

- **Vitamin C**: A powerful antioxidant found in citrus fruits, strawberries, bell peppers, and broccoli, Vitamin C is essential for repairing tissues, healing wounds, and aiding in iron absorption. It's also a powerful antioxidant that protects brain cells from damage.
- **B Vitamins**: Folate (B9), B6, and B12 are vital for brain health. Folate, found in spinach, asparagus, and Brussels

sprouts, is crucial for cell division and the production of DNA and RNA. B6, present in bananas, potatoes, and chickpeas, helps with neurotransmitter synthesis, affecting mood and sleep patterns. B12, found in dairy products and fortified cereals, maintains the sheaths that protect nerves.

- **Vitamin K**: Leafy greens like kale and spinach are rich in Vitamin K, which is known for its role in blood clotting and supports brain function by helping regulate calcium in the brain.

- **Vitamin E**: This antioxidant, found in nuts and seeds such as almonds and sunflower seeds, protects cell membranes from damage and is crucial for maintaining mental health and cognitive function.

- **Minerals**: Important minerals include iron, magnesium, and zinc. Iron, found in lentils and spinach, helps carry oxygen to the brain and is essential for cognitive development. Magnesium, present in avocados and nuts, is vital for nerve function and regulating neurotransmitters. Zinc, found in pumpkin seeds and peas, is crucial for brain growth and function.

By incorporating a colorful mix of fruits and vegetables into your diet, you're not just feeding your brain; you're building a foundation for overall health that supports everything from your immune system to your mental clarity.

ADEQUATE REST AND SLEEP

Sleep truly is the crown jewel of maintaining cognitive well-being. During those precious ZZZs, your brain busily sorts through the day's events, tucks memories into place, and processes emotions. Seeing rest as not just a physical need but as a vital investment in your mental clarity is key. Moments of simply sitting down and resting your body can also replenish your energy reserves, making you feel more rejuvenated.

Crafting a bedtime ritual that gently signals your brain that it's time to wind down can be incredibly helpful and helps ease you into a restful state, preparing you for a good night's sleep. Journaling, for instance, helps clear your mental space by putting thoughts on paper and relaxing your body, effectively using less energy and serving as another form of rest. And don't underestimate the power of a quick nap; even brief ones can act like a reset button for your mind, especially when nighttime sleep is choppy. So, while sleep may be elusive at times, you can aid your body's recovery by simply slowing down and allowing yourself to take ten minutes for a mental reset. This approach ensures you continue to support your mental and physical health, even on the busiest days.

MANAGING CHRONIC FATIGUE

New mothers often find themselves hosting an unwelcome visitor: never-ending fatigue. Not the tiredness that comes from staying up late for fun; it's a deep, bone-aching weariness that becomes a constant companion in the early days of motherhood. Chronic fatigue often feels like an unrelenting, pervasive sense of exhaustion that persists despite adequate rest. It's not just feeling tired after a busy day or a poor night's sleep; it's a profound and debilitating heaviness that can impact every aspect of daily life. Individuals experiencing chronic fatigue may describe it as an impenetrable, draining sensation that overwhelms even simple tasks. It's like navigating through thick fog, where mental clarity and physical energy are elusive. This fatigue can accompany other symptoms such as muscle aches, headaches, difficulty concentrating, and irritability. Chronic fatigue in new moms can stem from a mix of physical recovery, hormonal changes, and psychological adjustment to a dramatically altered lifestyle. The clue to recognizing chronic fatigue lies in its persistence and impact. While normal tiredness eases with rest, chronic fatigue stubbornly lingers, overshadowing moments of joy and dulling the vibrant experiences of new motherhood.

You can employ practical ways to boost your energy to lighten the burden of exhaustion. Nutrition, often sidelined in the demands of newborn care, is crucial. Incorporating foods rich in iron and B vitamins can give your body a boost. Eating small, frequent meals can also help keep your blood sugar levels stable, warding off the peaks and troughs that exacerbate tiredness. Staying hydrated is another simple yet effective strategy, particularly important for breastfeeding moms. A glass of water may seem mundane, but it's a simple act of self-care that consistently helps refresh your energy levels.

Gentle exercise offers a refreshing path to regaining your clarity. Whether it's a leisurely walk, a quick stretch session, or simply shaking your body, moving can help shift energy. You can run, hop, or bop in place—whatever feels good. Moving your body can help dispel the fog faster, giving you a renewed sense of coherence and an energy boost. Approach these activities not as part of a daily grind but as moments of self-care and rejuvenation.

However, restorative sleep is the most powerful way to combat fatigue. This elusive remedy, often interrupted by the needs of a newborn, is crucial to lifting the fog of tiredness. There are several strategies to improve sleep quality. Creating a calming bedtime environment and embracing the "sleep when the baby sleeps" mantra can make a significant difference. It's hard, but the more you do it, the more your body will want to sleep at that time. It's a good thing. Yes, many things need your attention, and tons of tasks are waiting to be done, but sleep anyway. Sleep through it all so that when your baby wakes up, you have energy for the most important task that overrides all others. You will have more patience, so the nurturing will be genuine, and that colossal list will seem manageable. We often view sleep as taking time away. In essence, it's giving us more quality time than running on empty ever would. So, how can you be kind to yourself right now? Remember, your body just grew a baby. You can sleep when the baby sleeps.

Memory Aids and Organization

In today's world, where smartphones often feel like an extension of our minds, using technology for organization and as a memory aid can help clear the mental fog. Creating lists can transform the overwhelming task of remembering everything into something completely manageable. Using calendars and reminders takes the pressure off your brain from having to keep track of appointments and tasks. Sound notifications can help keep you on point, too. Think of your device as your personal assistant, helping you navigate your day with less stress and more confidence. Moreover, many apps integrate seamlessly across your devices, ensuring you have access to your schedules, notes, and reminders at home or on the go. Embracing these tools can significantly enhance your daily productivity, allowing you to focus more on enjoying moments rather than managing them.

DEALING WITH ISOLATION AND LONELINESS

New motherhood holds surprises in every corner. One challenge that sneaks in quietly is isolation and loneliness. It often starts innocently enough, perhaps with the exhaustion of those sleepless nights or the endless cycle of feeding, changing diapers, and soothing your little one. At first, it might feel like just another part of the journey, something you'll eventually adjust to. But then, slowly but surely, it creeps in, wrapping around you like a heavy blanket.

Loneliness in new motherhood can feel like being adrift in a sea of uncertainty, surrounded by people yet feeling utterly alone. It's that pang of longing when you see other moms chatting happily at the park while you stand on the sidelines, unsure how to join in. It's the ache in your chest when the day stretches endlessly ahead, filled with nothing but the sound of your baby's cries and your thoughts. It's the quiet tears you shed in the darkness of night, wondering if anyone else feels as lost and overwhelmed as you do.

But here's the thing—you're not alone in feeling alone. Many new moms experience these same feelings, even if they don't always talk about them. That's why it's so important to reach out and connect with others who understand what you're going through. Even though it may seem like everyone else has it all together, the truth is that we're all just figuring it out as we go along.

So, if you're feeling isolated or lonely, know it's okay to reach out for help. Whether joining a new mom's group, scheduling a video call with a friend, or simply sharing your feelings with your partner, taking that first step toward connection can make all the difference. In the end, it's those moments of shared laughter, of knowing nods and understanding smiles that remind us we're never truly alone on this journey of motherhood.

Amid the joys and challenges, recognize that you're not just a mom but a whole person with your own needs, desires, and dreams. Be gentle with yourself. You're doing an incredible job and deserve a moment of care and compassion just as much as anyone else. Self-care doesn't have to be extravagant or time-consuming. Giving yourself permission to rest when you need it or setting boundaries to protect your time and energy, even the simplest acts of kindness toward yourself, can make a world of difference in how you feel. These little acts remind you that you're more than just a mom—you're a person with needs, too.

NAVIGATING BODY IMAGE AND SELF-ESTEEM

In today's social media-driven world, where everyone's life seems like a highlight reel, the pressure to live up to unrealistic post-partum recovery standards can be overwhelming. It casts a shadow over the authentic experience of motherhood. Maneuvering through this digital landscape requires wisdom and courage to shield oneself from comparisons that steal joy and chip away at self-esteem. Remember that those picture-perfect moments you see on social media are snapshots chosen, edited, and shared purposefully. Keeping this fact at the forefront can save you from feeling inadequate when comparing yourself to them. Instead, focus on finding real connections and communities where moms share their diverse experiences. In those genuine online and in-person connections, you'll find comfort and strength to build yourself up and be proud of who you've become. Body image is not just about your physical body; it's also about the strength of your mental health. Be your best supporter. Be your own best friend.

Body positivity is all about accepting and celebrating your body just as it is. It's about recognizing that everybody is unique and worthy of love and respect, regardless of size, shape, or appearance. By making small, daily choices and giving yourself positive affirmations, you're nurturing a healthy relationship with yourself. When those negative thoughts try to creep in, challenge them with reminders of your strengths and accomplishments. Surround yourself with positive influences, both online and in real life, that celebrate diversity and promote self-love. Remember, it's okay to have off days—we all do. That's where self-compassion comes in, treating yourself with kindness and understanding. Your postpartum body is a testament to your strength and love, not something to criticize. Embrace your body's journey and start being kind to yourself. That's when the healing begins, and you'll emerge feeling more robust, more confident, and totally unstoppable.

OVERCOMING BREASTFEEDING CHALLENGES

Starting your breastfeeding journey is a unique mix of challenges and rewarding moments. It's common for new moms to run into issues with latching, which is one of the first hurdles you may face. Getting the perfect latch is imperative to effective breastfeeding and involves finding the right angles and positions. It can be uncomfortable or even painful if it's not right. Ensure your baby's mouth covers a good portion of the areola below the nipple, not just the nipple itself, to avoid painful pinching and ensure your baby gets enough milk.

If you're constantly feeling pain during feedings, it could be a sign that the latch isn't quite right, which can sometimes lead to cracked or sore nipples. It may be a good idea to get advice from a lactation consultant. They're great at offering hands-on tips and showing you how to improve the latch.

Worries about milk supply are also common. Some moms have too much milk, which can lead to engorgement and a painful swelling of the breasts. Others may worry about insufficient milk, which can be stressful as it impacts your baby's growth and nourishment. Staying hydrated, eating a well-balanced diet, and getting enough rest can help manage these issues. But if you're still concerned about your milk supply, talking to a healthcare provider may be helpful.

Lactation consultants bring knowledge and empathy to the table, offering more than just practical advice—they provide a comforting presence that reassures moms, affirming that challenges can be navigated successfully with patience and care. Healthcare professionals also play a crucial role by using their expertise to identify and address any issues hindering successful breastfeeding. They may suggest pumping strategies, supplements, or other methods to help regulate or enhance milk production.

Additionally, consider joining parenting support groups. Whether they meet in hospital rooms, community centers, or online, these groups are valuable spaces where experiences are shared, understanding is mutual, and support is authentic. Support groups can be beneficial if you are navigating different feeding methods, have questions, or feel confused—they provide a reliable source of help and information.

Exploring different feeding methods involves discovering what works best for you and your baby. Sometimes, traditional breastfeeding may not go as planned, and that's perfectly understandable. Whether you choose bottle feeding with expressed breast milk or formula or even try out supplemental nursing systems, there are plenty of options to ensure your baby receives the nourishment they need. Each choice is deeply personal, shaped by your preferences, needs, and circumstances. Let's embrace the range of feeding methods without any judgment. The most important thing is that feeding time is a moment of nourishment and love for you and your baby.

Navigating the ups and downs of breastfeeding isn't just a physical challenge; it's an emotional rollercoaster, too. Wrestling with latch issues, wincing through pain, and fretting over milk supply can tug at your heartstrings, sprinkling your days with doubts and guilt. But it's so important to remember, amid all these challenges, to be kind to yourself. Struggles don't define your worth as a mom. Managing these intense emotions often means giving yourself a break—reminding yourself that perfection isn't the goal. Every day that you try your best is a victory in itself. So, take a deep breath, give yourself some grace, and recognize that just doing your best is truly something to be proud of.

UNDERSTANDING THE PELVIC FLOOR

The pelvic floor is a group of muscles and tissues that stretch like a hammock from the pubic bone at the front to the tailbone at the back. These muscles play a critical role in supporting the organs in the pelvis, including the bladder, intestines, and uterus in women. During childbirth, the pelvic floor muscles are significantly stretched, and sometimes they can be damaged or weakened, which is quite common.

When you give birth, especially vaginally, these muscles undergo a lot of strain. They help push the baby out and bear its weight during pregnancy. After birth, if the pelvic floor weakens, it can lead to several issues, such as urinary incontinence (difficulty controlling urine), pelvic organ prolapses (where pelvic organs drop and press against the vagina), and reduced sensation during sex.

Strengthening the pelvic floor after childbirth is crucial for several reasons. First, it helps restore muscle tone and strength, which can prevent the issues just mentioned. Second, a strong pelvic floor helps realign and stabilize your core, which is vital for overall strength and wellness postpartum. Lastly, these exercises can help speed up recovery after birth, making it easier to safely return to other forms of physical activity.

Exercises for Pelvic Floor Strengthening

Focusing on pelvic floor exercises, often called Kegel exercises, can be a significant aspect of postpartum recovery for new mothers. These exercises involve contracting and relaxing the pelvic floor muscles, which helps strengthen them and improve circulation to the area, aiding in healing. Regular and correctly performed pelvic floor exercises are pivotal to regaining strength and function in this area after childbirth.

To perform Kegel exercises, it's essential first to tune in to the feeling of engaging your pelvic floor muscles, similar to the sensation of stopping the flow of urine midstream. Once you've made this connection, the exercise involves a simple but effective pattern—contract these muscles for three to five seconds, then relax for a moment. You should repeat this rhythm of tension and release up to ten times per session, three times a day. Each repetition is a small but mighty act of resistance against the challenges of postpartum recovery, helping you rebuild strength quietly but effectively.

Breathing is a powerful tool for boosting pelvic floor vitality, with each breath allowing you to engage these crucial muscles.

Diaphragmatic breathing, which involves taking deep breaths that expand your belly, helps naturally sync your diaphragm with your pelvic floor muscles. This synchronization not only strengthens these muscles but also incorporates the calming rhythm of your breath into your recovery process.

You can try this exercise quickly.

1. Place one hand on your chest and one on your belly.
2. Contract your pelvic floor.
3. Breathe deeply through your nose, ensuring only the hand on your belly rises.
4. As you exhale, relax the pelvic floor.
5. Repeat.

This technique specifically targets and strengthens your pelvic floor muscles as you breathe. Aim to practice this a few times a week, or include it in your daily routine as it suits you. Remember to focus on belly breathing during this exercise. This simple yet effective practice can turn little moments into powerful opportunities for healing and strengthening.

These exercises aren't just about recovery; they're about empowering you to feel more confident and comfortable as you navigate this new chapter of life. Incorporate these exercises as they feel right for you, without pressure to make them a daily task. Every small effort contributes to your overall well-being, allowing you to heal and strengthen in a way that suits your body's needs and schedule. Remember, your journey is unique, and taking steps toward recovery should fit seamlessly into your life as a new mom, offering you the flexibility you need.

As we wrap up, remember that stepping into motherhood is a significant transition, full of highs and lows. Caring for yourself is not just a luxury; it's a fundamental necessity. Throughout this chapter, we've explored how to take care of your health after your baby's arrival, how to understand your body's needs, and the importance of seeking support when you need it. Remember, you're not alone in this journey—your feelings are normal, and prioritizing your well-being is crucial for you and your baby. Hold on to these tips as you move forward, be gentle with yourself, and rest assured that you're doing wonderfully. Welcome to the beautiful journey of motherhood—embrace it with all the love and courage you possess.

CHAPTER SEVEN

ADVANCED SELF-CARE AND GROWTH

Imagine yourself as a quiet place hidden beneath the energetic buzz of city life, essential yet often overlooked—much like your internal experiences as a new mom. While you're busy with your new baby, your emotions and thoughts might remain hidden, but they are incredibly important. Journaling is a way to tap into these hidden parts of yourself, providing a refreshing flow that helps sustain and nurture you during this particular time. Remember, journaling doesn't need to be time-consuming. Sometimes, just a couple of sentences can make you feel better. Let the words hit the page and create more space for you.

JOURNALING FOR EMOTIONAL RELEASE

Journaling is more than just writing things down; it's a conversation with yourself, a soothing ritual that peels back layers of stress to uncover the heart of turmoil and joy. Research supports its power in easing anxiety and helping us process our feelings. Writing out your thoughts and emotions is like setting them down on paper and stepping back, which helps clear your mind and manage your feelings better. This practice helps make sense of the intense emotions of new motherhood, offering a feeling of control and insight. Additionally, journaling can boost self-esteem by reflecting personal growth and achievements, provide a safe outlet for expressing unresolved emotions, and facilitate problem-solving by allowing different perspectives to emerge as you write. These benefits contribute significantly to emotional release, making journaling a valuable tool for mental health.

Prompted Journaling

For many, a blank page symbolizes potential yet stands as a daunting prospect. Prompted journaling bridges this gap, offering a starting point for exploration.

- Today, I felt...
- One thing I wish I could say...
- Today, I discovered...
- I cherish when...
- A small victory I celebrated today...

These prompts serve as guideposts, directing the flow of thoughts, making the blank page less intimidating, and inviting a structured reflection that unravels the complexity of day-to-day experiences.

Gratitude Journaling

Gratitude journaling is about recognizing and appreciating the big and small things in life, which can transform your outlook. It helps shift your focus from what's missing or stressful to what's fulfilling and joyous. Regularly writing down things like the

warmth of your baby's smile or a quiet moment alone encourages a mindset that seeks and values the positive, significantly
enhancing your mental health and perspective. Here are five
gratitude journal prompts to help you get started.

1. What was one moment today that made me smile?
2. Who made a difference in my day, however small,
    and how?
3. What am I learning from my challenges?
4. One comfort I enjoyed today that I often take for
    granted.
5. What was a peaceful moment in my day?

THERAPEUTIC WRITING

Therapeutic writing, a unique type of journaling, provides space
for unedited expression. It's where raw feelings, hidden fears, and
unnoticed triumphs can be freely voiced. This writing style isn't
about being eloquent or structured; its strength comes from being
genuine. It acts as a private retreat where thoughts and emotions
can be sorted out, explored, and made sense of, paving the way
for personal growth and healing. Consider these prompts to spark
your reflection.

1. What emotion did I feel most strongly today, and why?
2. Describe a moment today when I felt overwhelmed—
    what triggered it?
3. What small victory can I celebrate right now?
4. In what ways did I feel misunderstood today, and how
    did I handle that?
5. What am I most grateful for at this moment?

Here's a real one: Why am I so angry, irritated, and annoyed?

REFLECTIVE PRACTICES

Integrating reflective practices into journaling makes the process a rich source of personal growth. Reflection means revisiting past experiences with a critical but kind eye to identify patterns, triggers, and reactions. It involves questions like "Why did this moment affect me so deeply?" or "What can I learn from this experience?" This kind of introspection enhances self-awareness and offers insights that shape future thoughts and actions, building resilience and deepening understanding of oneself and the experience of motherhood. Here are five reflective writing prompts to help you dive deeper.

1. What surprised me today, and how did I react?
2. Reflect on a difficult moment from today. What emotions did it bring up, and why?
3. When did I feel most connected to my baby today, and what contributed to that feeling?
4. What was my hardest decision today, and what did I learn?
5. Describe a moment when I felt proud of myself today. What made it special?

Here's a real one: What happened today that I will never let happen again?

Journaling is more than just a simple activity—it can be a lifeline for a new mother. It offers a way to sort through the rich, complex mix of emotions and experiences that come with motherhood. Importantly, writing doesn't have to be extensive. As each mother narrates her own story, she connects with the deep well of her inner self, gaining clarity, strength, and a deeper bond with her transformative experience.

DAILY AFFIRMATIONS FOR STRENGTH

Days and nights can often blend into a continuous flow of caring for your little one, making it feel like there's no break in sight. Affirmations are simple yet powerful phrases that can genuinely transform your day. When you sprinkle them throughout your routine, they have the incredible ability to turn self-critical thoughts into empowering self-talk, uplifting your spirits and strengthening your resolve. The beauty of affirmations isn't just anecdotal; they're also backed by science. They activate the brain's pathways associated with positive thinking, boosting self-esteem and helping you recover from stress. Positive self-talk, like repeating affirmations, triggers the release of feel-good hormones such as dopamine and serotonin, enhancing your mood and offering long-term benefits for your mental health. So, when times get tough, keep smiling and repeat some positive affirmations.

Creating personal affirmations starts with a bit of soul-searching, diving deep into your own experiences and hurdles. This process means spotting those sneaky negative beliefs that tend to dim your moments of joy and achievement. Maybe it's that nagging inner critic doubting your mothering skills or a whisper suggesting you're not entirely up to par with others—these are the ghosts that affirmations aim to banish. Crafting affirmations is really about taking back the story of your life, stating loudly and proudly your worth, skills, and inner strength. For instance, an affirmation like "I am a loving and capable mother, even when I feel overwhelmed" is a pushback to doubt and a bold affirmation of your truth.

Weaving affirmations into your daily routine magnifies their effects, sinking these little gems of positivity deep into your subconscious. You might start your day with them during quiet morning moments, whispering affirmations like soft prayers that set a hopeful tone for what's ahead. Or use them as stabilizers during those tough times of stress or exhaustion, a mental sanctuary for quick refreshment and strength. Try sticking affirmations on visible spots, like a sticky note on your bathroom mirror or a reminder on your phone, keeping these empowering messages close at hand. Repeating these affirmations and thinking about their meanings can slowly transform your mental landscape, planting seeds of positivity that grow into a stronger, more resilient mindset.

For anyone starting with this transformative practice, here are a few examples of affirmations that might inspire and uplift you.

1. I am enough, just as I am today.
2. I trust in my ability to provide the love and care my baby needs.
3. Each day, I grow stronger and more confident in my role as a mother.
4. I give myself permission to rest when I need to, without guilt.
5. I celebrate each small victory, recognizing my progress.
6. I am surrounded by love and support, even on tough days.
7. I handle challenges with grace and patience.
8. I am learning and improving every day.
9. I focus on the joy and love that motherhood brings.
10. My journey is unique and perfectly tailored for me.

Affirmations reveal their true beauty through their adaptability and personal nature—you can modify and expand them as your life circumstances change. This flexibility ensures that your affirmations can grow and evolve with you, providing relevant support and inspiration every step of the way.

SELF-CARE FOR MENTAL CLARITY AND CALM

Self-care is crucial for keeping a clear mind and staying calm, especially for new parents navigating the complexities of caring for a baby. Taking care of your mental health is not just helpful—it's necessary. By prioritizing self-care, you ensure you stay resilient and continue to enjoy the journey of parenthood. Regular self-care also sharpens your thinking, helping you make better decisions and solve problems more effectively. Plus, it boosts your creativity, offering fresh perspectives and solutions for everyday challenges. Additionally, these self-care practices enhance your focus and concentration, which are vital when juggling the demands of parenting and personal life.

Leave the House

Stepping outside offers new moms a much-needed break from the constant demands of household chores and routines. Just stepping outside for a short while can feel incredibly refreshing. Being outdoors and engaging with the natural world provides a change of scenery, helps clear the mind, and restores mental balance. This break can be especially beneficial for reducing stress and promoting calm, making it easier to return to indoor responsibilities with renewed energy and a more relaxed perspective.

Finding time to enjoy the outdoors may seem like a challenge with everything motherhood throws, but it doesn't need to be a grand outing. A simple morning stroll in the park, with your baby in the stroller and the natural world around you, can be incredibly rewarding. Or spend an afternoon on a blanket under the open sky. Even sitting in your yard, hanging out on the stoop, or taking a quick walk around the block can be revitalizing. If you manage a five-minute outing before returning indoors, count it a success! Lower your expectations and be happy with whatever you achieve. It's not about the time spent outside but just the right amount of time to catch your breath. Use short excursions that allow you to breathe a little without straying far from home.

Relaxation through Reading

During those busy and joy-filled moments of taking care of your little one, grabbing a book can give your imagination a well-deserved break. For moms, reading a story can be a quick refuge from the demands of daily life, a gentle way to unwind. But if focusing on a book feels like too much, audiobooks are a fantastic alternative, allowing you to soak in the stories while you multitask or rest.

For those moments when even a short story feels too long, flipping through a magazine can offer quick, enjoyable diversions—perfect for when you have a few minutes to yourself. Consider a leisurely trip to the library to pick out a mix of books and magazines you can enjoy quickly. Reading doesn't have to be an intense commitment; it's all about finding little pockets of time, however brief they may be.

Sharing these reading moments with your baby makes them even more special. Even reading from your adult book aloud to your baby can be beneficial—they love hearing your voice, and it introduces them to the rhythms and sounds of language early on. The soothing rhythm of reading aloud, whether from a book or an audiobook, acts like a calming lullaby. Simple yet profound moments not only nurture a lifelong love for literature but also foster bonding time for you and your little one.

Hobbies in Self-Care

There will come a time when you can focus on your hobbies again. As your baby grows, you'll find pockets of space that allow your creative self to shine through. Hobbies are acts of creation and exploration, avenues to happiness that weave through your everyday routine. Engaging in a hobby affirms your self-worth, recognizing that amid caregiving duties, your joy and fulfillment are essential for overall happiness.

Hobbies provide a retreat filled with achievement and expression. They offer a way to channel stress into something tangible and beautiful. Incorporating hobbies into your self-care routine nourishes your spirit, enhancing your ability to care for others. It's a celebration of your identity, a reminder that within the caregiver is an individual brimming with passions and talents.

To make this easier, consider having a special place to keep your hobby materials for quick access. This way, you can easily pick up where you left off and quickly stow everything away when needed. This setup not only helps in keeping your living space organized but also ensures that you can seamlessly integrate your hobbies into your busy life as a new mom.

Guilt-Free Alone Time

While caring for everyone's needs, it's easy for your needs to get lost in the shuffle. That's why carving out some alone time is so precious, even though it can sometimes make you feel guilty. This guilt whispers of selfishness where there's only self-care. Embracing this time without remorse acknowledges its essential role, not as a luxury but as a vital part of well-being. Alone time is like the pause between words, a space to reconnect the dots, where your thoughts can roam free, and your soul can quietly express its needs.

It might come in the stillness of early morning in a quiet room, where you can reflect, free from the demands of others. Maybe late at night, as the world drifts to sleep, or within that breathing space during the day, when you can finally slow down. When claimed and savored, this cherished time becomes a source of renewal, offering a brief sanctuary that recharges you, enhancing your return to caregiving with fresh energy and clear vision. To enjoy alone time without guilt is to validate your own needs, understanding that by looking after yourself, you enhance your ability to care for others with more love, presence, and patience. Give yourself a moment of your precious time.

MINDFUL MOMENTS WITH YOUR BABY

Integrating mindful moments into your daily routine with your baby can significantly enhance your bond and bring peace to both of your lives. Simple mindfulness exercises and focused breathing are potent tools that effectively calm the mind and heighten awareness. These activities create a serene environment, deepening your connection and enriching everyday interactions. Most importantly, they play a crucial role in reducing stress and strengthening the emotional bond between you and your baby.

Often seen as a solo endeavor, mindfulness gains new depth when shared with your little one. It transforms routine tasks into rich opportunities for connection, making each moment intentional and attentive. For example, feeding, typically watched over by the clock, becomes a mindful practice when you fully immerse yourself in the present. Feel your baby's weight in your arms and notice the softness of their skin and the gentle rhythm of their feeding. Let these tactile moments ground you in the now, turning a routine feeding into a deep bonding experience.

During playtime, mindfulness opens the door to a magical world of discovery, seen through your baby's eyes. Sit with your little one on the floor, away from the distractions of phones and to-do lists. Observe their amazement at different textures and colors, sharing their curiosity and excitement. This joint exploration boosts your baby's sensory skills and enhances your presence, anchoring you both in the simple beauty of the present moment.

Bedtime, too, can become a mindful practice, transforming the end of the day into a serene ritual. Maintain a calm environment and a relaxed demeanor as you prepare your baby for sleep. Be fully present with each step of your bedtime routine, whether a warm bath or a gentle massage. Notice how your baby responds to soothing touches and the room's quietness. Sing or hum softly, feeling each note resonate between you. This practice helps settle your baby and allows you to wind down, making the transition to sleep peaceful and meaningful for both of you.

Breathing Exercises

The simple act of breathing, often automatic and unnoticed, becomes a profound source of calm for you and your baby when done mindfully. Engaging in straightforward breathing exercises can help synchronize your rhythms, easing the strain of sleepless nights and hectic days. Sit comfortably with your baby nestled against you, their head resting near your heart. Inhale deeply, drawing in the fresh, quiet strength of air, our life force, and exhale slowly, letting go of any tension and worries. Let your baby feel the gentle rise and fall of your chest. As you breathe in, embrace all your emotions, thoughts, and everything else happening around you. Then, as you slowly exhale through your mouth, let it all go. Feel yourself get fully grounded. Feel your baby's weight in your arms, and continue with slow, intentional breaths, practicing gratitude and cherishing this precious moment. Create a serene oasis, a moment of peace and strength you and your baby can draw from, anchoring you in calmness and connection. These moments of shared breathing promote tranquility and teach your baby a vital life skill—how to manage emotions through the soothing rhythm of breath.

Observing and Describing

The world is a magical place through the fresh eyes of your baby, filled with daily wonders. A leaf drifting to the ground, the playful dance of shadows from swaying branches, or a bubble popping unexpectedly—each moment is an adventure and a chance to practice mindfulness. For instance, you could describe everything you see to your baby, from colors and shapes to the purpose of an object and its spatial relationships, like near or far and front or back. Take your baby outside, or cozy up by a window where you can watch nature's ongoing show. Describe what you see in a gentle stream of words that captures your baby's attention. "See the red bird, baby? Watch how it hops from branch to branch, bright against the blue sky." These colorful descriptions help develop your baby's language skills and enhance your focus, where observing brings joy and wonder.

You could also describe different sounds that you hear—distinguishing between an ambulance and a car or the sounds in your immediate environment. Listening adds a rich layer to your experiences. As you tune in to distant sounds like a bell or the soft rumble of a train, you engage your auditory senses, sharpening your attention. Explain these sounds to your baby. As they grow, continue this practice to help develop their senses and awareness.

Focusing on sight and sound lets you stay fully present and trains your "attention muscles," enhancing your ability to concentrate. By intentionally observing and listening, you reinforce your mental clarity. Each sensory detail helps anchor you more deeply in the moment, transforming everyday observations into profound learning experiences and connections for both of you.

Mindfulness is more than just ticking boxes on a to-do list—it's a heartfelt journey that uplifts your everyday moments. It's about turning daily routines into meaningful experiences filled with calm, connection, and gratitude. Sharing moments of gratitude with your baby can transform simple daily activities into cherished memories.

Take a few quiet minutes daily to express your appreciation for your baby. You may mention how much you appreciate their hugs, the sound of their giggles, or the peaceful moments you share. This reflection deepens your gratitude and communicates to your little one how much they are valued. These small expressions of thanks enhance your mindfulness practice and strengthen the emotional bond with your baby, helping you celebrate the present and look forward to the future with love.

Balancing Baby's Needs with Your Own

Each day unfolds with the promise and challenges of nurturing a new life. Balancing your needs with your baby's needs becomes a subtle dance guided by intuition and deliberate action. Within this delicate balance, acknowledging and honoring your needs isn't self-indulgence but a crucial aspect of comprehensive care. Recognizing when you need rest, nourishment, or just a moment to yourself is essential. By caring for yourself, you ensure that you nurture your baby from a place of strength and abundance rather than exhaustion and depletion. This approach supports your well-being and empowers you to provide the best care for your little one.

It's important to remember that routines are not rigid schedules but rather flexible guidelines. They act as a sturdy yet adaptable framework to help manage the unpredictable rhythms of life with a baby. These tailored routines provide a rough plan for each day, merging your baby's daily patterns with your own. This balance of energy, attention, and care is crucial. Routines pave the way for feeding, play, rest, and those precious bonding moments. The real strength of routines lies in their adaptability, which allows you to seamlessly adjust to ever-changing circumstances.

At the core of balancing your needs with your baby's is the steady rhythm of self-compassion, which underlies every effort to nurture both of you. Self-compassion offers whispers of patience during moments of frustration, grants understanding when exhaustion sets in, and provides encouragement when doubts arise. It gently reminds you that seeking perfection in motherhood is chasing an unattainable mirage, distracting from the natural beauty found in the imperfect, the messy, and the genuine. Self-compassion permits mistakes, appreciates every attempt, and recognizes that each instance of imbalance presents a chance to learn, grow, and adjust. This kind-hearted approach helps you navigate motherhood with grace and understanding.

Recognizing your needs as valid and essential, seamlessly integrating your baby's rhythms into your life, and establishing adaptable routines create an atmosphere where love and understanding take the front seat, allowing joy to flourish throughout your days. Fostering self-compassion enhances the well-being of both mother and child and promotes a nurturing environment. How can you be kind to yourself and to your child today?

CHAPTER EIGHT

DAILY RITUALS AND RESILIENCE

S elf-care is as personal as your favorite cozy sweater or the perfect cup of tea. Imagine you're surrounded by jars of different blends in a tea shop. There's calming chamomile, vibrant peppermint, and everything in between. Choosing the right blend isn't about right or wrong; it's about what feels right in the moment, what soothes or energizes you. Just like picking your tea, self-care should match your taste, lifestyle, and the rhythm of your days. It's not a one-size-fits-all routine but a custom fit that snugly wraps around your life, wants, and daily reality.

Turning everyday self-care tasks into cherished rituals can make them feel almost magical, transforming the ordinary into moments of true significance. Take making a cup of tea, for example. It seems simple—just water, heat, and tea leaves. But when you do it mindfully, this simple act becomes a soothing ritual. You choose your tea, listen for the boil, watch the steam rise, and then savor that first comforting sip. When done daily, this simple act becomes a welcomed calming strategy. Treating self-care routines as precious moments turns them into more than just tasks on your list—they become grounding, peaceful pauses that anchor you in the now.

Integrating self-care into your daily routine is all about small, consistent steps. No matter how minor it may appear, every little action creates a baseline for your days. Self-care doesn't have to be about big gestures or extended hours. You can find it in the brief, quiet moments—taking a deep breath amid a hectic day, stretching gently in the morning sun, or enjoying a piece of chocolate in peaceful solitude. These simple acts of caring for yourself quietly and consistently foster resilience, enhancing your ability to handle life's challenges with grace, strength, and a tad more patience.

The unpredictable rhythm of motherhood demands flexibility, requiring you to adapt to your children's ever-shifting needs, schedules, and moods. Similarly, your self-care routine must embody this flexibility to truly benefit you. Some days, you might yearn for a vigorous workout; on others, something soothing and slow may feel right. The key is to tune in to your body, adjusting your practice accordingly and allowing it to nourish you without adhering to a strict regimen.

Your self-care should also be adaptable, fitting into the snippets of time you find, always aiming to uplift and support you rather than adding to your tasks. Engaging in self-care daily, or as often as possible, transforms it into a ritual over time. Your mind begins to anticipate and prioritize this practice, creating the mental space needed for its fulfillment. This awareness fosters a sense of ritual, an understanding of its importance for your continued health and performance. Even if you miss a session, acknowledging your needs and desires and knowing that you can create space for them will alleviate stress.

PERSONAL PEACE: CREATING YOUR IDEAL SELF-CARE RITUAL

Creating a self-care ritual that respects your personal needs, preferences, and the realities of daily life can transform your routine into a predictable yet flexible sanctuary of well-being. Here's how you can weave self-care seamlessly into your daily and weekly schedule:

- While making breakfast, prepare your afternoon snack, nurturing yourself before you need it.
- Brew a hot beverage. Once done, your reward could be to enjoy your drink fully (sit down) before moving on to the next task.
- When the baby is content or napping, take two minutes each day to stretch your body, reviving your energy or preparing you for a restful nap yourself.
- Dedicate Wednesdays for a stroller walk with your baby, combining fresh air and exercise.
- Choose the same day each week to do all your errands to help streamline your tasks and manage your time more effectively.
- Once a month, enjoy an outing with your family. Have a picnic, walk around the mall, take a car ride, etc.
- Before stepping out of the shower, take a long, deep breath and stand still for 30 seconds, giving yourself a moment of calm.
- Twice a week, indulge in an audiobook chapter, allowing yourself a literary escape.

These are just examples. Intentionally craft your routines to fit your lifestyle and situation. By making your self-care routine predictable and adaptable, you create more than just a list of tasks; you develop a source of strength and a pathway to personal well-being. This approach acknowledges that while your schedule may never be set in stone, having a flexible plan can make managing unpredictability easier.

USE PERSONAL GROUNDING TOOLS

Use the skills you learned in this book to structure your day. During breakfast, whether it's yours or the baby's, take a moment to reflect. Think about everything you need to do today (or this week), what's on your mind, who you need to connect with, and so on. Then, do a Brain Dump—this means writing down all your thoughts, tasks, and concerns on paper without any specific order. You'll immediately feel lighter. Next, identify your top priority. What is that thing you're determined to accomplish? (Maybe one day you will give yourself the luxury of accomplishing nothing on the list.) Then, choose one self-care ritual to pamper yourself with. Consider when you might find the time for it or decide when to make time for it.

For instance, list everything that is siphoning your mental energy. Choose one thing that will get done today. "Today, I am sweeping the kitchen right after lunch." This simple act of completing a task can bring a sense of accomplishment and motivation. Pick one thing that absolutely will get done this week. "I will call Glenn and tell her thank you for the gift she gave to the baby. I will call her before Thursday." If Thursday rolls around and you still need to do it, drop what you are doing and make the call, no matter what. Cross it off the list. If you don't, time will continue to go by, and you will feel guilty when you see her next because you haven't thanked her yet. Stay one step ahead of the guilt trip. What self-care practice will you incorporate into your day? "Today, I am going to wash my hair and cut my toenails, and if I have the energy or the time, I will do a face mask." "Today, I am going to tell my partner that I need a minute to recharge, and after they get home, I am going for a walk around the block all by myself." "I don't have time for myself today because I have all these errands to run, but tomorrow, I am going to eat a peanut butter and jelly sandwich and have a cup of tea." (I love peanut butter and jelly sandwiches.)

As part of your routine, incorporate gratitude by asking yourself, "Who loves me?" and "Who do I love?" Think of this phrase as a form of meditation. By doing it daily, you develop the mental strength to focus and create a framework of structure.

Meditation, in its various forms, offers a path to heightened awareness. It centers your mind, calms the nervous system, and cultivates inner peace that can shape your day. Engaging in a Brain Dump activity or journaling in the morning can also be a potent tool for setting intentions. The blank page becomes a canvas for your inner thoughts and feelings, providing an outlet and a mirror of your inner self. Through reflection, you gain clarity, establish your intentions, and prepare to approach the day with focus and grace. Acknowledging your thoughts can effectively maintain your mental focus and centered awareness.

Throughout the day, use your calendar, notifications, and to-do list apps and update them as needed so you don't have to keep remembering things. When you encounter indecision, pause and tune in to your body. How does your body feel with a Yes answer? How do you feel about a No answer? Sometimes, it might feel like a Maybe, but it's possible to immediately sense whether your body agrees or disagrees with a situation. Feel free to say no if that's the case. Recognize that the Yes/No exercise helps you establish your boundaries. Be gentle with yourself and reduce stress by tuning in to your inner voice.

If you feel overwhelmed, distracted, confused, or lost at any point during the day, try focusing your attention on one object. Fully immerse yourself in that moment and train your attention on that object. See its solidity, its edges, its color, and its shape. Tune in to its weight. Once it has your complete attention, bring your focus back to yourself. Take a deep breath in and out. Feel yourself grounding. Repeat this process as often as needed. Afterward, identify the one top priority you need to address at that moment. Whether it's making a phone call, drinking some water, attending to the baby, taking a moment to breathe fresh air, using the restroom, or jotting down a grocery item—take care of that one task. Then, identify the next top priority that needs your attention. If that's how you need to function for the next ten minutes, then consider it a job well done. Do whatever you need to do, however you need to do it. And if you find yourself lacking the energy to do one more thing, ask yourself, "How can I be kind to myself right now?" Most times, the answer will be, "Just take a seat, even if it's just for a minute." Do yourself a favor and do that.

Ending your day with positive affirmations is a comforting practice that helps your mind accept situations, come to terms with events, and reinforce your values. It can also promote relaxation, encourage better sleep quality, and cultivate a sense of gratitude for the day's experiences. Positive affirmations are a nurturing form of self-care, deeply tending to your mental and emotional well-being while fostering a positive mindset for the following day. Examples of affirmations include statements like "I am grateful for everything I learned today," "I trust in the guidance of my inner voice," and "I am deserving of love and happiness." A very empowering and resonant affirmation is "I did my best."

Taking just a few minutes daily to practice mindfulness can make a difference. It can help shift energy by reducing stress and lifting your overall mood. It nurtures self-love, equipping you with more patience and a positive outlook that enriches your bonding time with your baby, filling it with more kindness and care.

CHAPTER NINE

NURTURING YOUR RELATIONSHIPS

Building and nurturing relationships is like tending to a garden—it takes time, effort, and lots of love. Whether it's your connection with your partner, family, or friends, these relationships are the backbone of your life. They're what make the good times great and the tough times bearable. And just like a garden, relationships need regular care and attention to flourish. So, let's roll up our sleeves and dig into some tips for nurturing those bonds and keeping them strong and healthy.

THE ART OF COMMUNICATION

In the tender early days of parenthood, our closest relationships transform. This shift in your relationship with your partner calls for a special kind of care—a blend of understanding, patience, and teamwork that forges an even stronger bond. Remember, you're in this together, sharing the joys and challenges of parenthood, and that shared responsibility can make the journey less overwhelming.

Communication is the lifeline of your connection. It's how you navigate this journey together, ensuring your relationship remains solid and supportive as you embrace the joys and challenges of parenthood. Effective communication ties us together and can heal any divides when we speak and listen with respect. This shared language of love and responsibility, constructed through sharing needs, expectations, and feelings, sets the tone for new parenthood. Your voice is important and should always be heard and respected.

When managing tasks like coordinating nighttime feedings or planning weekend activities, the key lies in how clearly and openly we communicate. It's not just about expressing your needs; it's about doing so in a way that fosters teamwork rather than conflict. Transparent, open communication is essential because it builds a foundation for teamwork. By voicing your needs effectively, you can strengthen your bonds and ensure that these conversations lead to cooperation instead of tension. Here are a few examples of effective communication in action.

- **Nighttime Comfort**: If one partner handles most of the baby soothing during the night, an open conversation could go something like this. "I've noticed that I've been feeling worn down lately. Getting up with the baby every night is starting to wear on me. Could we discuss how I could get some extra help during those times? Maybe you could take over soothing the baby to sleep after I feed her."
- **Weekend Plans**: When planning weekend activities, instead of one person deciding for the family, it could go like "What do you think about going to the park this Saturday? I thought getting some fresh air together

might be nice, but I'm open to other ideas if you have any!"

- **Household Responsibilities**: If chores are piling up, discussing them without assigning blame could look like, "I've noticed the laundry is piling up, and we're both pretty busy. Maybe we can set a time this weekend to tackle it together? It always feels more manageable when we do it as a team."

- **Personal Time**: If one partner needs more time to themselves, a considerate way to bring it up might be, "I love our family time, but I'm feeling a bit run down. Could I take a few hours for myself this weekend? Maybe you could have some bonding time with the baby, and I could recharge a bit."

Couples who see their interactions as opportunities to grow together view teamwork as fertile ground. In this environment, mutual support and understanding flourish, strengthening their partnership with each challenge. Regular check-ins can be considered tending to a garden, ensuring the soil is rich, the weeds are pulled, and the plants thrive. These moments of connection—whether sharing a cup of tea after the baby's asleep or going for a walk as a family—provide a chance to discuss the changes they're both experiencing, building empathy and fortifying their bond.

Healthy relationships thrive on boundaries and realistic expectations. These boundaries are seen as gentle guides, not barriers, creating a secure space for individuals to blossom separately and together. By openly discussing personal time, shared duties, and emotional support, couples lay the groundwork for a relationship that flourishes even amid the challenges of parenthood. Setting boundaries is not about control but rather empowering each other to thrive in this new phase of life.

SHARED PARENTING

Through shared parenting, flexibility and adaptability take center stage. This ever-shifting landscape calls for both partners to stay nimble, ready to swap roles and tasks at a moment's notice. In this fluidity of acceptance, unexpected strengths often emerge—finding patience in the early hours or a talent for bedtime stories that soothe a restless child to sleep. The key is letting these roles evolve naturally, without rigid expectations, knowing that the flow of daily life may call for changes in responsibilities, always with your child's well-being in mind.

Disagreements are inevitable, but finding common ground becomes crucial in these moments of conflict. Navigating these disagreements requires a balance of standing your ground and finding compromises, whether they stem from different parenting styles or the nitty-gritty of daily decisions. Imagine one parent prefers strict routines while the other loves the freedom of unplanned days. The solution isn't about one side winning but about finding a middle ground that respects both perspectives and keeps the family's well-being in focus. This pursuit of harmony, fostered through open conversations and mutual respect, strengthens the family against the potential strains of conflict, knitting them into a more resilient and united unit.

Valuing each other's need for personal time sets a strong foundation for a healthy relationship. It's about recognizing that each partner deserves moments of peace and solitude, whether for rest, fun, or simply to catch their breath. This mutual respect acknowledges that each individual maintains their identity and needs, even within the partnership. By honoring this concept, partners recharge and nurture a relationship built on respect and empathy. Imagine one partner stepping in to handle childcare duties so the other can have some uninterrupted self-care time; it's a small yet powerful gesture that strengthens their bond with kindness and love.

Showing appreciation and acknowledgment is like sprinkling magic dust, making everything sparkle a little brighter. It means recognizing the little things—the extra mile walked, the chores done without being asked, and the love woven into every task. When we express gratitude for these efforts, it's like watering a garden, ensuring that no gesture of kindness goes unnoticed and that resentment doesn't take root. A simple thank you, a sweet note, or a loving word can turn ordinary moments into precious reminders of love. This culture of appreciation, nurtured with care, helps the relationship navigate parenting challenges with grace and understanding.

A masterpiece of unrivaled beauty and strength takes shape with shared parenting, where flexibility, adaptability, mutual respect, and appreciation are the colorful threads. It's a delightful testament to the power of partnership amid the ups and downs of parenting, reminding us that together, we can tackle any challenge with a smile and savor every joy even more sweetly.

THE ROLE OF FAMILY AND FRIENDS IN YOUR SUPPORT NETWORK

Moments shared with loved ones are a wonderful chance to catch your breath and be yourself. Whether it's a cozy dinner with family or a quick catch-up over coffee with friends, these simple moments remind you that there's more to life than just parenting. They reconnect you with the person you were before the sleepless nights and endless diaper changes, reigniting passions and interests that you had paused. These gatherings remind you of the many hats you wear—friend, sibling, child—each adding a layer to your identity. So, don't forget to make time for these relationships even when you feel too busy. These connections will strengthen your bonds with others and give you the emotional boost you need to tackle whatever parenting throws your way.

Entering the world of parenthood is like going on a rollercoaster ride. For some, it's thrilling. For others, it's terrifying. In both cases, it is full of unexpected twists and turns. And thankfully, you don't have to navigate this wild journey alone. Your support network, composed of family and friends who've got your back, help to hold and keep you steady. You can lean on your network when things get tough, celebrate when things go right, and share the messy, beautiful experience of parenthood.

Building and nurturing a support network is essential. Open communication is key, allowing you to share the ups and downs of parenting and family life. Keep the dialogue flowing so you don't feel like you are doing this alone. Regular catch-ups help keep those connections strong. And don't forget to involve your loved ones in your child's milestones—they'll love being a part of those special moments and will shower your little one with love and affection.

Including your family and friends enriches these experiences and deepens your connection within your support network. Asking for help when needed is not a sign of weakness—it's a sign of strength. It shows that you know your limitations and are willing to reach out for help when you need it most. Don't hesitate to lean on your support network when the going gets tough. Whether it's a listening ear, a helping hand, or just some sage advice, your loved ones are there for you, ready to lift you and help you through the challenges of parenthood.

MAKING NEW FRIENDS AS A NEW MOM

The comfort of companionship is that familiar feeling of sitting down with a trusted friend, knowing you're not alone in your experiences and that someone is there to listen, understand, and share your journey. Mom groups, in particular, often become a lifeline—a community of voices resonating with one another's fears, dreams, and victories, forming a chorus of support and inspiration.

These gatherings offer more than parenting tips or commiseration over sleepless nights; they create a sense of belonging. Whether meeting in cozy homes or lively parks, people swap stories, give guidance, and fill the air with laughter. This feeling of belonging becomes a source of assurance, reminding us that we're not alone in our struggles and that the joys of motherhood are even sweeter when shared.

When looking for places to connect with other moms, there are plenty of options out there! Local community centers often host parent and baby groups, which can be a great start. Libraries sometimes offer story times and other parent-child events, which can also be wonderful opportunities to meet other moms. Online, you can look for parenting forums or social media groups specific to your area. These can be incredibly convenient, especially when leaving the house is a big task. Lastly, consider asking your pediatrician or your child's healthcare provider—they often know about local mom groups and can provide recommendations.

Mom groups are wonderfully diverse, bringing together a rich mix of experiences, parenting styles, and viewpoints. This variety enriches the group, though it also means you'll encounter a wide range of opinions and approaches. To thrive in these settings, it's important to approach each interaction with empathy and an open mind, recognizing that while each mother's journey is unique, common feelings of hope, fear, and love bind us all.

Maintaining healthy boundaries is essential in the close-knit community of mom groups, much like in other areas of life. These boundaries act as personal guidelines, defining our comfort zones and promoting mutual respect, ensuring that group interactions remain positive and fulfilling. They necessitate the ability to respectfully decline, refrain from passing judgment, and bravely step back if conversations take a negative turn. By establishing and upholding these boundaries, we protect our well-being and contribute to the overall health and positivity of the group, preserving it as a supportive and nurturing space for all members.

Engaging in constructive conversations focusing on under-standing rather than convincing can also create a supportive and nurturing environment. The strength of mom groups truly emerges when everyone embraces their differences and finds common ground in their shared experiences.

The magic of forging genuine connections within mom groups lies in small acts of kindness. It flourishes in moments of vulnera-bility, where barriers come down and hearts open up to reveal motherhood's raw, authentic essence. These connections, grounded in authenticity and mutual understanding, can provide companionship and support when it's needed most.

In conclusion, remember that each relationship is a vital part of your support system, whether it's with your partner, your friends, or fellow moms. Like any good garden, these relationships need your attention and care to thrive. Take the time to nurture these connections, communicate openly, and share your journey. These bonds enrich your life and provide a strong foundation as you navigate the ups and downs of parenthood. But remember, it's not just about nurturing; it's about being nurtured, too. Reaching out for support when you need it is a sign of strength, not weakness. It's together—with the support and love of those around you—that you'll find the strength and joy to flourish in the beautiful, challenging adventure of motherhood.

CHAPTER TEN

EMBRACING CHANGE - THE ONLY CONSTANT IN MOTHERHOOD

As the soft morning light streams through the curtains, a mother awakens to a completely transformed world. Her life, once defined by predictable routines, now moves to the spontaneous rhythms of her newborn's demands. Amid moments of calm and chaos, change becomes a constant presence—essential and unexpectedly filled with beautiful moments. Every day brings new shifts that she navigates with grace, finding beauty in the unexpected and learning from each new challenge.

Motherhood brings a profound transformation. It's a deep, irreversible change filled with both challenges and triumphs. Embracing change isn't simply about letting things happen; it's about understanding and finding strength. Every sleepless night and unpredictable day adds depth and color to your life. Navigating life's transitions, from the early days with a newborn to the challenging teenage years, is like walking on shifting sands—unpredictable yet full of potential. Each phase brings its own set of challenges and joys, continually reshaping family life. Consider the milestone of moving from exclusive breastfeeding to introducing solid foods. Amid the messy faces and scattered crumbs, there's laughter, discovery, and a growing sense of independence. It's a vibrant illustration that transitions are about coping with change and embracing and celebrating growth. Embracing these moments means staying present, responsive, and gentle with yourself as you and your child explore new adventures together.

It's common to feel as though the threads of your pre-motherhood self have become tangled or lost. Yet, despite these feelings, your core identity remains. It's all about weaving the passions and pursuits that define you into your new life as a parent. If you loved running before, now it might mean jogging with a stroller or enjoying a long walk at your child's pace. These adaptations allow your identity to evolve beautifully. Embrace the fluctuations of motherhood, knowing that each change presents an opportunity for resilience and beauty to emerge.

Transforming everyday tasks into acts of self-care is about the intention behind each action. When carried out with love and mindfulness, these small deeds integrate self-care seamlessly into your daily routine, nurturing your body and soul. This approach turns routine moments into opportunities for self-expression and well-being. Remember, mindfulness can be brief or extended, depending on what suits you daily. Your ability to stay present will change based on your energy, priorities, and the challenges you face. Strive for what feels manageable daily. The more you practice the mindfulness exercises from this book, the more easily and quickly you'll reconnect with yourself, enhancing your overall well-being.

Taking a moment to pause and reflect is incredibly valuable. It helps you recognize your growth as a reflection of your patience and dedication. Each act of self-care is a step toward achieving a more balanced self. By acknowledging these actions, you give them meaning, transforming simple tasks into significant milestones in your journey.

Incorporating a gratitude practice into your routine can enhance this process. Imagine maintaining a journal where each page is a canvas for your daily triumphs. Every entry, like a brushstroke, adds color and depth to the story of your journey. This simple yet profound practice creates a space where progress is recognized and celebrated. It shifts your focus from what remains to be done to the beauty of what you have achieved, fostering a mindset where gratitude flourishes, enriching your soul with fulfillment and peace.

Recognizing and celebrating each small triumph is crucial to self-care. When pieced together, these moments can influence your day and your entire life. From noting progress to celebrating achievements, these actions accumulate, creating a journey of resilience and strength. As you navigate through the different phases of motherhood, each victory in self-care enriches your experience, steering you toward a greater sense of balance and fulfillment. This ongoing journey emphasizes that even minor steps can lead to significant, life-enhancing changes.

REVISING YOUR SELF-CARE GOALS

In those quiet moments when life offers a pause, there's a perfect opportunity for self-reflection. In doing so, consider whether your current self-care routines are still serving you well or need some tweaking. As our lives change, our needs and goals evolve too. That's why it's important to reassess our routines occasionally. Instead of rigidly sticking to a set plan, adapting these practices to fit our changing circumstances can make them more effective and personally fulfilling. This flexibility ensures that your self-care evolves harmoniously with your life's transitions.

While routines provide a sense of security and predictability, it's equally important to incorporate regular check-ins to adjust and rejuvenate your self-care practices. These moments of introspection allow you to gauge the effectiveness of your self-care routine. What once served you well may now require a refresh or a replacement. Trusting your instincts and making necessary adjustments is a key aspect of personal growth. Adapting your self-care doesn't necessitate a complete overhaul of your life; often, it's about recognizing what no longer serves you as circumstances change. This trust in your own judgment is a powerful tool in your self-care journey.

Embracing adaptability is a testament to your resilience, enabling you to develop new self-care practices that better align with your current self, not your past self. This is particularly relevant in the first five years of your child's life—a period of immense change —where cultivating a mindset of flexibility and openness can significantly boost your well-being. This approach not only aids in managing personal stress but also in fostering a nurturing environment for both you and your child.

As we wrap up this chapter, we see that self-care is an ongoing journey, constantly evolving and adapting. It's a reminder that taking care of yourself is never a fixed routine but a dynamic process that requires regular reassessment and openness to change. For new moms, this journey requires deep self-reflection, the ability to adapt, and a readiness to make changes based on feedback and personal insights. Committing to this continuous cycle of improvement with honesty and courage will enhance your well-being and positively impact everyone around you.

CONCLUSION

Here we are at the end of our journey together. What a ride it's been, right? From those first moments of holding your baby (and probably a fair amount of your hair in frustration) to now, you've transformed in ways you probably never imagined. You've evolved emotionally, mentally, physically, and even spiritually.

You've learned your new mantra, "How can I be kind to myself today?" can create an awareness of your immediate needs and wants and can easily be the center of your new self-care routine. Remember, taking care of yourself isn't just a luxury; it's an integral part of the beautiful, transformative process of becoming a new mom. We've covered everything from clearing your head and assessing your priorities to finding the proper self-care practices that resonate with your lifestyle. We've tackled mental health, physical well-being, and family communication, incorporating empathy for yourself and others throughout the process.

We discussed the importance of listening to your body and nurturing it back to health gently and with compassion. Being centered and grounded will assist you through the inevitable challenges that arise. Remember, self-care is as unique as you are. It's not a one-size-fits-all kind of deal. It's about making the strategies and activities we've discussed work for you. Your life, your rules.

Use the tools and exercises to streamline your days and reduce stress. More calmness within you leads to greater bonding with your little one. Make space for you and your baby so that the world revolves around you instead of the other way around. Lean on your support group whenever necessary, and know that you are loved enough to do so. It takes a village, a community, an understanding pet—anyone and everyone on Team You.

There will be days when you grieve the spontaneous you, struggle with your reflection in the mirror, or feel like you're failing because your house doesn't look like those Instagram feeds. And that's okay. You're now equipped with the tools, the understanding, and the awareness to navigate these instances with more grace than you realize.

So, what's the next step? Start small. Feeling overwhelmed? Do a brain dump. Feeling anxious? List your top priority. Are you feeling blue? Journal it out. Too much going on? Focus your attention. These skills are here to help you get through the tough times. The more you do it, the easier it will get. It's about progress, not perfection.

To each incredible, resilient, perfectly imperfect mom reading this: You are doing a fantastic job. The fact that you're even thinking about self-care amid the whirlwind of motherhood is a testament to your strength and love. Keep exploring, adjusting, and, most importantly, being kind to yourself. The journey of motherhood and self-care is ongoing, ever-changing, and always rewarding.

As we close this chapter together, I want you to carry a deep sense of belief and trust in yourself. Motherhood is transformative, and caring for yourself is a powerful act of love—not just for you but your family. I hope this book has been more than just a guide; I hope it's been a companion and a support on your incredible journey. Here's to embracing a future where self-care is as intuitive and heartfelt as your love for your little one.

Special Resource for New Moms

As you navigate the beautiful and often challenging journey of new motherhood, it's important to remember that you're not alone. To support you along the way, we've created a special resource: "Embrace Your Journey: Daily Affirmations for the New Mom." This collection of carefully selected affirmations is designed to uplift, inspire, and strengthen you during this transformative time.

Whether you're seeking a morning boost, a moment of peace during naptime, or a comforting thought at the end of a long day, these affirmations are here to help you find balance and joy in your new role as a mom.

We invite you to download this free PDF and incorporate these affirmations into your daily routine. They can be read aloud, written in a journal, or simply reflected upon to provide daily encouragement.

Download your free PDF: https://bookhip.com/NRPSRQM

Embrace these moments with love and positivity, and remember —you are doing an incredible job.

With warmth and support,

Sharlene Hosek

PREPARING FOR AN INCREDIBLE ADVENTURE

Self-care is your fuel as you advance through every thrilling stage of motherhood, and you're going to need it. This is your moment to remind other new moms that self-care isn't a luxury – it's a necessity.

Simply by sharing your honest opinion of this book and a little about your own experience of implementing self-care strategies as a new mother, you'll give other moms that much-needed reminder.

Thank you so much for your support. Motherhood is the best adventure we'll ever get to go on... but every one of us needs these self-care strategies to make the most of it.

Scan the QR code to leave your review on Amazon.

APPENDIX

FIND SUPPORT: LIST OF NATIONAL GOVERNMENT AGENCIES

For those navigating the early stages of motherhood, or any stage for that matter, knowing where to turn for support can be a lifeline. Below, a compiled list of national government agencies stands ready to help. Please check with your State Agencies for local resources.

Health and Human Services (HHS): At the forefront, HHS provides a broad spectrum of health-related resources, from healthcare coverage options to nutritional assistance programs. Their website is a hub of information on child welfare, mental health support, and preventative health services, vital for mothers seeking guidance and support.

- Toll-Free Number: 1-877-696-6775
- Website: www.hhs.gov

Centers for Medicare & Medicaid Services (CMS): For questions about healthcare coverage, CMS offers detailed explanations of options available through Medicare and Medicaid, including coverage for children and postpartum care. Their resources are indispensable for mothers navigating the complexities of health insurance to ensure their families receive the care they need.

- Toll-Free Number: 1-800-633-4227
- Website: www.cms.gov

Women, Infants, and Children (WIC): Specializing in the nutritional needs of mothers and young children, WIC aids with food, health care referrals, and information on healthy eating. Their services are particularly valuable for low-income pregnant women, breastfeeding mothers, and children under five, offering not just resources but a community of support.

- Toll-Free Number: 1-800-522-5006
- Website: www.fns.usda.gov/wic

Office on Women's Health (OWH): OWH serves as a comprehensive resource on women's health issues, including postpartum depression and breastfeeding support. Their initiatives and programs offer education, support, and a platform for women to connect and share experiences, fostering a community of understanding and assistance.

- Toll-Free Number: 1-800-994-9662
- Website: www.womenshealth.gov

Early Head Start and Head Start Programs: Focused on the early development of children from low-income families, these programs provide educational, nutritional, and parental support. For mothers seeking early childhood education and development resources, these programs offer a foundation for growth and learning, preparing children for future success.

- Toll-Free Number: 1-866-763-6481
- Website: www.childcare.gov

BIBLIOGRAPHY

Affirmations for Creatives and Makers - JOURNAL. (n.d.). Nicky Allen. https://www.nickyallen.co.uk/journal/a-daily-routine-using-affirmations

Asw, C. T. (2024, February 25). *30 Positive Affirmations for Moms: Embrace Motherhood with Self-Compassion and Positivity With Daily Affirmations.* Living Openhearted. https://www.livingopenhearted.com/post/mom-affirmations

Boosting your milk supply: Tips and STRA | Maternally. (n.d.). Maternally. https://www.maternallyapp.com/boosting-your-milk-supply-tips-and-stra

Borkowska, A. (2024, March 3). *Postpartum Recovery More Important Than "Six-Pack."* GentleWoman Polska. https://gentlewoman.eu/en/postpartum-recovery-more-important-than-six-pack/

Centre of Perinatal Excellence (COPE). (2023, October 29). *Postnatal Rage - COPE.* COPE. https://www.cope.org.au/new-parents/first-weeks/postpartum-rage/

Cypress Wellness Center. (2023, October 9). *Pelvic Health & Intimacy During Pregnancy: What You Need to Know.* Cypress Wellness. https://www.cypresswellnesscenter.com/post/pelvic-health-intimacy-during-pregnancy-what-you-need-to-know

Dobrivoje. (2024, April 16). *80 Positive Affirmations for Evening: Evening Euphony.* Positive Affirmations. https://positiveaffirmationscenter.com/affirmations-for-evening/

Fluker, C. (2024, February 11). *A Simple Guide to Get Started with Prayer Journaling.* WhatCherithInks. https://whatcherithinks.com/prayer-journaling/

Garone, S. (2019, September 26). *We asked sleep consultants how to survive the newborn days.* Healthline. https://www.healthline.com/health/sleep-consultants-share-tips-for-new-parents

Nct. (2023, November 20). *How to communicate with your partner after having a baby | Life as a parent, Your relationship as a couple articles & support.* NCT (National Childbirth Trust). https://www.nct.org.uk/life-parent/your-relationship-couple/relationship-challenges-and-support/how-communicate-your-partner-after-having-baby

Pascarella, S. (2023, November 1). *The Power of Connection: 7 Benefits of Joining MOM groups and support networks.* Wash With Water. https://www.washwithwatercare.com/blogs/news/the-power-of-connection-7-benefits-of-joining-mom-groups-and-support-networks

Postpartum Depression - Symptoms and Causes - Mayo Clinic. (2022, November 24).

Mayo Clinic. https://www.mayoclinic.org/diseases-conditions/postpartum-depression/symptoms-causes/syc-20376617

Rice, A. (2024, January 8). *Recovering from Delivery (Postpartum Recovery)*. familydoctor.org. https://familydoctor.org/recovering-from-delivery/

Smith, M., MA. (2024, February 5). *Gratitude: The Benefits and How to Practice It*. HelpGuide.org.   https://www.helpguide.org/articles/mental-health/gratitude.htm

Voice of Flower. (2023, November 15). *Postpartum Massage | Postpartum Repair | Voice of Flower*. Voice of Flower - Confinement Care Center. https://voiceofflower.com/postpartum-massage/

Yeh, Kristi. *23 Self-Care Quotes for Parents*. Parent Self Care. https://parentselfcare.com/blog/23-self-care-quotes-for-parents